"As the CEO of a busy organization, I fall into the category of the boss who tends to be a little daunted with all things of an IT nature. Often when communicating with IT support personnel, I get the strange feeling that we are not speaking the same language! David Papp's common-sense advice certainly helps to demystify the IT world and assists in planning for current and future IT needs. This is a must read for all business owners and provides a wealth of information delivered in an easy-to-read format."

Chris Lawrence
President and CEO
Better Business Bureau of Central & Northern Alberta

"David Papp's *IT Survival Guide* provides insight into the culture and inner workings of the IT department and provides practical and common-sense recommendations for corporate managers to better understand how to maximize the benefit of their IT infrastructure investment. This book is an enjoyable read. It is written in a fashion that appeals to both nontechnical people and techies alike, and it contains information that is easily applicable to any size organization."

Jason S. Lueke, Ph.D., PEng
Assistant Professor
Arizona State University

IT Survival Guide
Conquering Information Technology in Your Organization

David Papp

PFH Publishing

IT Survival Guide
Conquering Information Technology in Your Organization
Copyright © 2011 by David Papp
PFH Publishing

For more information: publishing@davidpapp.com

Printed in Canada

IT Survival Guide
Conquering Information Technology in Your Organization
David Papp

Library and Archives Canada Cataloguing in Publication

Papp, David
    IT survival guide / David Papp.

ISBN 978-0-9868213-0-1

    1. Information technology--Management. 2. Information resources management. 3. Emergency management. I. Title.

HD30.2.P36 2011   658.4'038   C2011-900169-1

To my wife and children,
who are most precious to me.

The only source of knowledge is experience.
—Albert Einstein

)

IMPORTANT!

The author has endeavored to be as comprehensive, current, and accurate as is possible. Most topics are based on the personal experiences of the author, which may differ from the average.

This book does not purport to offer legal, investment, accounting, computer, engineering, or other professional advice. If and when such expert counsel is required, the services of a competent professional should be sought. The author and publisher are not liable for loss or damage alleged to be caused directly or indirectly by information contained in this book.

As always, the best advice is: *caveat emptor;* BUYER BEWARE!

TABLE OF CONTENTS

ACKNOWLEDGEMENTS

I would like to thank my parents for buying our family computers; the past BBS community; the university engineering computer lab with Internet access; my family for allowing me to continue doing what I enjoy; my wife for encouraging me to write this book; Doug, Jason, Greg, Phil, Marc, and everyone I have ever been in touch with who teach me something new each time.

Technology is fun and has become my career.

INTRODUCTION

A major corporation developed a serious problem with its IT system. Each of the IT managers had tried repeatedly to figure out why the system was operating poorly but could not find the solution. After a critical deadline was missed, the executives made the decision to call upon an IT consultant to assess their situation. The consultant walked into the main data center where the servers were located, paused for a moment, and then placed a large "X" on one of the machines. "This is your problem," he stated and then left as quickly as he had come.

A week later, the company received an invoice for $10,000. Outraged, the CFO sent a letter to the consultant demanding an itemized account of the invoice. A few days later came an itemized invoice that contained only two items: "Placing an X cost $1. Knowing where to place the X cost $9,999."

While many versions of this story exist, its value still highlights the importance of having both specific and general knowledge. The IT managers of the corporation certainly had expertise in their IT system but likely lacked enough knowledge to step back and see the problem. Others in the organization, such as the executive staff, probably lacked enough specific expertise to understand the essence of the problem from the start. The consultant, however, had both the ability to understand specifics about IT troubleshooting and a wide scope of experience about IT systems in general that allowed him to efficiently diagnose the problem.

From this viewpoint, an IT consultant can be viewed as a general contractor with the skill set necessary to solve complex problems. Not only do IT consultants understand detailed aspects of information technology systems, but they also can appreciate a more comprehensive perspective. The ability to focus on the problem rather than being distracted by the symptoms allows them to identify a solution.

Unfortunately, too many organizations have executives and IT personnel who share a limited understanding of their IT environment. This may be caused by a number of factors. Executives often see information technology as a necessary evil, as the cost and financial demands often leave a bad taste in their mouths. If you combine this with a relative lack of "soft" skills common among many IT managers, executives rarely fully appreciate how they can benefit from effective IT structures.

Other times, IT managers may choose to withhold information about IT systems, falsely believing that this provides some degree of job security. If no one else knows how an IT system is configured, then their value within the organization is presumed to be higher. Both of these behaviors lead to miscommunication and misinformation about IT systems; as a result, the organization is less able to compete and achieve success in the end.

My goal as an IT consultant has therefore been to help bridge this gap between executives and IT managers while enlightening both about more-effective and more-efficient IT systems. Likewise, this is the purpose of this book. As a type of general contractor, I assess organizations' information technology situations from global and specific viewpoints alike to offer the simplest solution that achieves the goals, missions, and values of the organization.

IT systems do not have to be complicated. In fact, simpler systems enable more-efficient troubleshooting, and this results in fewer problems over time. This realization often brings a great deal of relief to an organization's executives, who can now grasp how their information technology networks operate. It also pleases IT managers, who subsequently find their jobs less complicated.

I began my career as a consultant during my teenage years. My family had purchased a computer when I was young, and despite its black-and-white monitor, basic cassette drive, and limited processing speed, my love for computer technology was almost immediate. Before long we upgraded to floppy disks, then to a hard drive (5 megabytes!), and I began to gain more customers as friends and family members purchased computers. Mine was a true basement operation; I assembled and repaired computers under the name Hardwired Computer Systems. By the time I was ready to graduate high school, I had earned enough money consulting that I purchased my own PC with a state-of-the-art Intel 386dx running at an incredible 33 MHz speed. I was on top of the world.

From there, I began experimenting with bulletin board systems and gained an interest in file networking. Though modems and networks were clearly in their earlier, more-primitive states, the ability they offered to one user to connect with other users remotely and to share files and programs was very intriguing. In 1991, I was accepted into the engineering department at the University of Alberta. Although I secured a good foundation in engineering concepts, I also furthered my knowledge in computing sciences and electrical engineering through electives. During this time I first encountered the Internet. I transferred a file through the Internet from a server in Japan without incurring any costs whatsoever. It was at this moment that I realized internetworking (as well as the Internet) was the wave of the future. Nothing else came close to it in terms of information access, communication, and functionality. As a result, I decided to obtain a degree in computer engineering, and I have been hooked ever since.

With this passion, I continued to perform information technology consulting services. For some organizations, I serve as a technology advisor who educates them about their IT needs and provides simple yet effective solutions to keep them competitive.

For larger organizations, I offer the same services in addition to serving a variety of other roles. For example, I may serve as a one-time troubleshooter to identify and solve a specific problem, or I may perform periodic IT assessments and audits to gauge the ongoing health of the organization. In today's business climate, IT is an integral and important part of most organizations' operations.

Different organizations have different needs. Having the opportunity to see a variety of IT systems as well as different IT challenges gives IT consultants a unique advantage. Unlike representatives of specific brands (such as Cisco ™ or Microsoft ™), consultants see multitudes of different IT products and systems. And unlike an organization's IT manager who experiences the same system every day, consultants enjoy a variety of challenges from many different organizations' systems.

Through my experience in the field of information technology I have come to realize that many organizations need a better understanding of how information technology can be of benefit to them. This naturally involves the organizations' executive staffs but also pertains to IT managers as well. By devising straightforward solutions and conceptualizing IT systems in simplistic terms, both groups can come together in a greater understanding of information technology in general. This allows alignment of values and goals between the organization and the IT department, and this promotes quality investments in resources for everyone's benefit. As a general IT contractor, I hope to provide this level of understanding while simultaneously bridging any gaps in communication between an organization's executives and its IT personnel. When everyone is on the same page, efforts as well as resources can be utilized more effectively.

The ultimate purpose of this book is to provide a basic knowledge about information technologies, IT tools, and IT systems. In addition, by understanding the purpose of IT assessments and periodic IT consultation, organizations can determine if these services may be of benefit in the short term as well as over the long haul. I also hope to reveal common limitations among executives and IT personnel as these pertain to miscommunication and misinformation about IT matters. Once these aspects are put forth, remedies and solutions are offered to help put your organization back on track. IT is without question a key aspect of an organization's success today and into the future. Investing time and effort into understanding how IT can best serve you is not only a wise investment but one that is likely essential if your organization is going to succeed.

CHAPTER ONE

Today's Information Technology Environment: Putting out Fires

It's Monday morning, and everyone is returning to his or her desk or cubicle from a nice, relaxing, leisurely weekend. Among them is John, a trepid fellow who heads the IT department. He casually rides the elevator to the third floor where he expects to step into his normal routine. But this Monday is different (or perhaps unfortunately not), it seems. John is immediately greeted by several colleagues, and his phone begins to ring nonstop in the background. Apparently the server had been down for the entire weekend, and no one can communicate within or from outside of the organization. The office is in panic. Fortunately, John is well equipped to handle such a catastrophe…or is he?

As have many information technology managers, John inherited his job almost by default. When he began working for the company twelve years earlier, he mentioned that he had taken a course in Microsoft technologies and was certified in one of the company's products. That was enough for the company owner to place John in charge of all technical issues. The company was quite small at the time John started but has since nearly tripled in size. Despite John's dedication to quality performance, the task of staying abreast of all the changes in IT has become overwhelming for him to manage by himself. Rather than being able to plan ahead for the company's IT needs, he has become a firefighter, fixing many small problems as they arise. Each week, several IT "fires" would be brought to his attention, and one by one he would try to extinguish them. Handling a company's information technology in this manner was far from ideal.

Unfortunately, many organizations have people just like John managing their IT departments. A lack of standardization in management qualifications, a rapidly expanding field, and a lack of appreciation of IT in general contribute to the problem. Business owners and executives do not understand the importance of budgeting for IT expenditures nor the variety of components in the IT department that likely require attention from other professionals.

Conversely, IT managers often lack the soft skills needed to explain this importance in practical terms. As a result, preventative maintenance, upgrades, and assessments of the organization's information technology are neglected, being either outright ignored or put off until time becomes available. The only time IT issues are considered is when a malfunction occurs in daily operations. By then, the problem has likely snowballed into a much bigger issue that will cost the company resources, bottom-line dollars, and client loyalty!

So where does the problem lie? Is it John's fault for not staying abreast of what the company needs and pushing for IT financial allowances to accomplish them? Perhaps the company's executives and/or owners are to blame for their shortsightedness regarding the importance of investing in information technology. Most of the time, a combination of these factors are at the heart of the matter. And with such a rapidly expanding field, an inherent lack of understanding and knowledge of current technologies is always present to some degree. Therefore executives, owners, and IT professionals must understand the importance of information technology and its value to an organization. Without this realization, the company will move from one fire to the next, handicapping its ability to grow and succeed.

The Evolution of Information Technology

In 1984, approximately 1,000 Internet-connected devices existed in the world. Today, this figure far exceeds 1 billion devices[1]. Text messaging was nonexistent until 1992, but now the number of daily text messages sent and received around the world surpasses the entire world population[2]. While these figures are astounding, the amount of cumulative information is also growing at an exponential rate. The amount of information published in just one week of *The New York Times* is believed to be more information than a person living in the eighteenth century would have acquired throughout his or her entire life. In addition, the amount of new information generated this year will be more than the information generated in the last 5,000 years combined. Specifically, the amount of documented technical information is doubling every year. Students enrolled in technical-educational programs learn information their first year that is obsolete by their last year. Is it any wonder that an IT manager or business owner may have difficulty grasping the latest IT trends and needs?

I like to compare the field of information technology to the field of construction. As we have developed better methods of construction and have employed newer technologies that enable more efficiency and higher quality, subspecialization becomes critical. The plumber no longer knows the best way to lay and grout tile. The electrician does not know all the latest features of various security systems. Even the general contractor must be regularly educated about new techniques and materials in certain specialty areas. The same applies to the fields of medicine, law, and even accounting. As the availability and volume of information has exploded, a demand for subspecialization has evolved in several disciplines, and information technology is no different.

As an IT consultant, I have seen an entire gamut of network and security catastrophes. For some organizations, the personnel in charge of information technology have only a limited scope of knowledge. Their ability to manage complex issues, much less keep up with new developments, may be insufficient, and as a result, over time, servers and hard drives begin to crash as capacity is reached or backups fail. All too often I conduct an IT assessment for an organization only to find that someone has either ignored or neglected obvious warnings that the IT system was at risk. In some cases, ignorance was to blame; in others, the IT staff was simply too busy handling emergencies to employ maintenance or preventative measures.

About ten years ago I received a call from the owner of a small company regarding a problem with remote access to its network. A telecommunications company that provided remote-access ability for the company had washed its corporate hands of the problem, stating that they were not to blame. At the same time, the company's IT department had reviewed and reassessed everything without finding a cause of the problem. This difficulty had been intermittently ongoing for more than a year. After visiting the IT department and reviewing its remote-access network, I identified minor problems on both sides that accounted for their issues. Within four hours the issue was solved, and everyone was pleased that there was finally a solution to the problem.

While these types of "magical fixes" are not common for such a long-standing issue, this experience demonstrated how subspecialization is needed in the information technology field. Neither the telecommunications company nor the in-house IT staff understood the nuances of the remote-access system. Training, educational updates, and ongoing curriculums are essential parts of the IT field, but even so, no one can be knowledgeable about every detail. This is where IT consultants can be extremely valuable to an organization. They have the time to learn cutting-edge information; this knowledge can routinely save organizations time, money, and frustration.

Subspecialization indeed provides an ability to exhibit advanced knowledge in a particular area. However, being an expert in information technology also allows one to envision the broader scope of an organization's network and IT system. In this regard I consider myself an IT general contractor. Not only can I understand the individual "trees" but can also view the "forest" as a whole. In what I like to call the "Stuck in a Box" syndrome, I get to see inside other people's boxes and share those experiences. In part this ability stems from my ability to view an organization's processes as an outside observer. Because I am not involved in the day-to-day, month-after-month, year-after-year operations, I can step back and view the organization from a macro perspective. This ability, combined with subspecialized knowledge, allows me to more-readily identify unforeseen problems and potential concerns.

For example, one client I assisted had developed over many years multiple software applications housed in a series of servers. Several different vendors had helped develop these applications with my client during this time, and multiple in-house personnel had been involved in the development as well. Thousands of hours had been invested in this company's online product content, yet the client had little understanding of the company's IT systems. When a problem arose, the company's owners did not know where to turn for help. The big picture had so many components that an IT general contractor who had knowledge of web servers, web development, programming, and a variety of other technologies was required just to assess the problem. Even with this knowledge, it still took a couple of months before a complete backup of configuration files and content as well as a recovery recipe could be devised to solve the root of the problem. None of the experts previously involved had the ability to see the big picture, and as a result, the company was put at risk for losing all its years of hard work.

We are living in exponential times in regards to growth of information technology. New developments that are occurring on an annual basis simply dwarf the developments in prior centuries. With this being understood, the need for IT subspecialization and ongoing education is imperative. You wouldn't want a family doctor performing open-heart surgery; likewise, you shouldn't want a junior IT staff person managing the complex array of servers, networks, backups, and firewalls your organization relies upon. IT systems make or break organizations every day in our global, competitive marketplace. Taking the time to invest in your IT infrastructure and system is crucial, and it takes asking only a few questions to start heading in the right direction.

A Few Questions Every Organization Should Consider

The problem in dealing with a topic such as information technology lies in its complexity. Rapid expansion and a constant state of flux makes it difficult for business owners, executives, and even IT managers to know exactly what problems might exist. How can you prevent a catastrophe if you are not even aware of your current IT abilities? In an initial discovery meeting, a few specific questions can help direct everyone to focus on the area in which limitations or problems might lie. Even if specific answers are lacking, the absence of knowledge may by itself point to areas of concern.

1. **Have any operational mishaps or warning signals been noticed?**

   Many times, slowing of normal operations goes unnoticed in an organization as the capacity of memory, storage, network, or processing reaches maximum levels. Illuminated lights may change from green to orange or red, indicating an issue of capacity. If a standard mechanism by which these observations are made, recorded, and addressed are not in place, these warnings can be ignored. As a result, catastrophes most likely will occur, and once again, IT managers are forced to put out fires instead of focusing on more-important tasks.

2. Who are the key IT personnel, and what ongoing training do they receive?

If an IT manager exists for the organization, a serious examination of his or her qualifications, ongoing training, and performance activities should be considered. Many times, junior IT personnel with limited knowledge and training are placed in senior positions over time despite lacking some of the needed skills and expertise. Many options exist to improve these situations.

3. What documentation regarding IT is performed?

Where are passwords and documentation for file servers, email servers, workstations, backups, and other IT assets located? Is a logging system in place? How often is it examined for issues, trends, and functionality? Are IT personnel recording documentation and changes appropriately? Is documentation stored on-site, off-site, or both? These can become very important questions if a disaster occurs or if personnel difficulties arise.

4. Where are the key storage areas for backups and archives?

Are storage areas located on-site, off-site, or both? Is a centralized storage area network used, or is local storage utilized? In addition to the type and location of storage being utilized, the frequency of backups and archives is also important and should align with the organization's operations and philosophies.

5. Where are key resources and staff located?

Resources can involve workstations, file servers, email servers, shared applications, and much more. Where these items are located can be important. What if a fire occurred in an organization's primary site? Are adequate resources located in other areas to allow for business continuity? Likewise, are accommodations for staff available in other locations in case of a localized IT failure? Location plays a big role in many IT system analyses.

6. What happens if a system failure occurs after hours?

As Murphy's Law states, catastrophes will occur at the most inopportune time. Too many times I have seen a system failure or crash occur on a Friday evening after business hours. As a result, business operations are offline the entire weekend until someone finally realizes it Monday morning. What if an important backup or update was routinely scheduled on the weekend? Understanding the repercussions of such a failure and whether alerts should be in place is a very appropriate question to ask about your business.

7. How do your clients or suppliers respond if no one answers communications?

No one wants to experience this scenario, but the question highlights the risks involved should business continuity become interrupted or not properly function. In a competitive industry, customers and clients will often turn to a competitor if poor communications exist. Likewise, partners and suppliers may view your organization as disorganized or unprofessional and question your ability to deliver. It is important to have IT systems in place that preserve operations and communications in the event that disaster strikes.

8. How often are updates performed?

Some statistics have been given already that demonstrate the rapidity with which information technology is expanding and changing today. Therefore, processes and procedures that address routine updates and upgrades to existing IT systems and applications are worth considering for implementation. Efficiency, effectiveness, and growth of the organization can all be negatively affected if these areas are ignored. And, more important, the cost associated with major overhauls to rebuild infrastructure as opposed to scheduled upgrades can be substantial.

9. What protections are in place if a power outage occurs?

Most organizations have some kind of battery backup power supply should electrical outages occur, but the extent and duration of alternative power may be inadequate to provide proper business continuity. The use of battery backups, generators, and power monitors are common topics that surface during discovery meetings with IT professionals. In addition, how power is managed can save significantly on energy utilization and costs.

10. How often are outside assessments and audits performed?

No matter how much expertise and experience your organization's IT personnel have, a fresh perspective always has the chance to reveal new opportunities and potential issues. This exercise can reap significant rewards particularly in the field of information technology.

Conducting an IT assessment of your organization with outside professionals offers you a chance to identify areas that could be improved that internal personnel may not see. New methods and techniques specific to IT management and systems develop almost daily. External assessments are the best way to tap into the latest trends and applications so that your organization maintains its competitive advantage.

Though the questions listed here are often asked during an initial discovery meeting between business owners, IT managers, and a consultant, these meetings are typically very organic and fluid. A single question may take the group in a direction that highlights the urgent needs of the organization. However, the above list does show common areas in information technology that commonly become major problems for a number of organizations. Unfortunately, once you fall behind and begin putting out fires instead of maximizing performance, resources within the organization are often focused on survival rather than on success.

A Step in the Right Direction

Perhaps you are like John with a crisis on your hands, or perhaps you have considered the questions listed above and realized that you have shortcomings within your IT organization. Either way, a systematic and organized examination of your organization's information technology systems and operations needs to be conducted to start the process. For many larger organizations, this may be attempted in-house, but as mentioned previously, a fresh perspective is extremely valuable. This is where the services of an IT consultant become very helpful.

The initial step is to arrange a meeting with an IT consultant who can help identify potential problem areas. This is most commonly called a "discovery meeting" for obvious reasons. For my clients, these meetings are informally structured so that issues and concerns will easily surface. General questions are asked, and if problems are identified, then follow-up questions become more specific and directed at relevant areas. Conducting on-site tours of the functional areas and data centers may also reveal other areas of concern. These meetings often require just a couple of hours and can yield a substantial amount of information and insight.

During constrained economic times and robust economic cycles alike, organizations often have difficulty spending time and money on IT development and maintenance. I see very few organizations that have a dedicated budget allocated to information technology itself. Instead, they throw money toward IT only when urgencies or emergencies occur. By then, the costs of fixing a problem as opposed to preventing it in the first place have escalated significantly. Choosing to assess and audit your IT department operations is without question a step in the right direction financially for the organization.

Finding a qualified IT consultant (especially one who fits well with your organization) is important and often difficult. Qualifications and certifications are far from standardized within the industry, as will be highlighted later in this book. In addition, this individual will have access to some of your organization's most valuable information. This person should not only be someone with whom you can easily interact but also someone whom you can completely trust. Some pointers in selecting an IT consultant will be covered in the subsequent chapter, but in general, word-of-mouth referrals are often the most reliable.

In the following chapters of this book, areas of information technology that may be of concern will be covered in much greater detail. In fact, many additional areas not yet mentioned will also be covered. Whether you are a business owner, executive, or IT manager, these topics will help you understand the importance of properly managing IT systems. In addition, the benefits of periodic external assessments and audits of IT operations can be realized. These low-cost exercises in preventative maintenance can save tremendous amounts of time and money in the long run for your organization. With today's exponential growth of technological advances, the decision to invest in IT for your organization is clearly the right decision.

References
1   Internet Devices: http://newsroom.cisco.com/dlls/2009/corp_121009.html
2   Text Messaging: http://en.wikipedia.org/wiki/Text_messaging

CHAPTER 2

Getting Started:
Conducting an IT Assessment

So where does an organization begin when it considers evaluating its information technology systems? Commonly, everyone in the IT department has been so overwhelmed trying to keep his or her head above water that no one has a good grasp of the current situation, much less the future IT needs of the organization. Likewise, the owners and business executives are unaware of the latest trends within information technology and would prefer not to spend potential profit dollars on systems and processes that may not be needed. When this is the situation, conducting an IT assessment is certainly a step in the right direction.

But what exactly is an IT assessment? An information technology assessment is a formal examination of an organization's current abilities in managing information. The initial scope is quite broad and includes areas such as network and storage capacity, memory and processing availability, backups and archiving, monitoring and alerts, and much more. Depending on the size and complexity of your business, these areas can encompass a wide range of considerations. Therefore, an IT assessment varies significantly in scope according to your specific organization.

When a situation exists in which in-house IT managers and business executives are not sure where information technology problems may lie, IT assessments generally begin as a broad overview of current practices, processes, and capacities. As areas of concern are identified, a more detailed analysis is then performed, providing more-specific information. This method of investigation benefits everyone. Providing a thorough snapshot of the current IT situation in a short amount of time can allow key issues to be targeted without a tremendous investment in resources. Decisions can then be made based on the level of importance and desired level of risk to determine if a more thorough investigation into specific areas is required.

The bottom line is that an IT assessment is the initial step in determining whether an organization's IT system is healthy or whether significant risks exist. This process can be performed within the organization, as it often is, or with the help of outside IT consultation. Outside consultation with professional experts offers not only a fresh perspective but also a subspecialized analytic ability that in-house managers may lack. Either way, periodic IT assessments are strongly recommended in order to allow an organization to stay abreast of rapidly changing developments in information technology. Once the decision to pursue an IT assessment has been made, arranging a preliminary meeting, known as the discovery meeting, is the next task at hand.

The Discovery Meeting

To summarize its main purpose, a discovery meeting serves to identify what an organization needs in terms of its information technology systems. Commonly, a discovery meeting lasts only a couple of hours and entails a generalized question-and-answer session guided by a facilitator. The facilitator may be an expert in information technology within the organization, or the facilitator may be an outside IT consultant. In the process of asking questions and collecting answers, important and sometimes critical issues are uncovered that reveal areas of weakness or concern.

Though the agenda for a discovery meeting is fairly loose and open-ended, some basic areas are always addressed. Processes and procedures essential to the smooth functioning of both present and future operations are examined. Is the organization prepared to handle a sudden information disaster? In the event of a disaster, will business continuity be preserved and maintain seamless transitions in daily functions? These questions touch on the most crucial aspects of information technology for any business and can lead to specific areas of concern rather quickly. I have conducted discovery meetings on several occasions during which serious risks in these areas were identified within the first few minutes. Many clients have even confided that they recently experienced some form of a disaster situation.

Among the many topics discussed, disaster recovery is perhaps the most important and the most common. What happens if a hard drive crashes, power is lost, or a network connection fails? What happens if a server becomes nonfunctional, a database is corrupted, or a fire engulfs a main office building? Disaster recovery refers to short-term crises that are acute and potentially catastrophic. Response time, disaster detection, and resource allocation are just a few hot topics that need to be addressed as part of a disaster-recovery plan. Unfortunately, many organizations have no such plan, and when disaster does strike, the worst is experienced.

On equal footing with disaster recovery is the ability to maintain business continuity in light of a catastrophe. If disaster recovery is viewed as an acute plan to restore normalcy, business continuity represents the long-term ability to continue operations almost seamlessly while the disaster is being addressed. Despite being integrally related and interdependent, disaster recovery and business continuity represent different strategies and address different problems. An organization with proper business-continuity strategies in place can keep clients, vendors, partners, and sometimes even organizational members from being aware that a disaster has even occurred. In other words, business-continuity strategies allow an organization to buy time while disaster-recovery measures are employed.

One common concern about such discovery meetings involves determining which organizational members should attend. In addition to IT managers and chief technology and information officers, who else should be present? From my perspective, the presence of business owners as well as the chief executive staff is often quite valuable at discovery meetings. While it is not imperative that they attend, their perspective on the importance of smooth operations, risk aversion, and resource investment tends to make the meetings more productive. For example, IT managers may feel password, network, and process documentation is not critically important to the organization perhaps because hoarding this information provides a false sense of job security for them. In contrast, a CEO may feel entirely different, realizing the risk involved if this information is lost should something happen to key IT individuals. Having everyone who shares interest in proper IT operations at the discovery meeting allows for a unified direction to be quickly defined. This in turn enhances the productivity of the meeting.

The other benefit to having executive and ownership members present at a discovery meeting pertains to the allocation of financial resources. I often consult with organizations that are resistant to investing monies into IT systems. Executives can fail to see the benefit of addressing these issues before catastrophe strikes, especially if IT managers lack the communication and business skills needed to present the pros and cons of an IT budget in an understandable manner. However, when executives attend a discovery meeting during which issues are explained in practical terms and financial investments that mitigate risk can be justified, their opinions can change. When they gain this level of understanding, it can make a significant difference in the proposed plans at the end of the meeting, and often funds can be quickly obtained from other budget areas of the organization.

A few years ago, a colleague of mine referred a client for an IT assessment. My friend made me aware from the start that the organization was resistant to spending any money on IT development and viewed it as an inconvenient expense. And when they contacted me, one of the first questions asked was what value they could expect for the money spent on my services. Rather than trying to justify everything up front, my approach was to simply suggest a two-hour discovery meeting. Overall, this was a minor expense, and the client was agreeable to this initial step. In fact, the client placed the cost of the meeting on a credit card using discretionary business funds.

As it turned out, the meeting revealed several important issues that needed immediate attention. In addition, I was able to provide many simple inexpensive suggestions, including some free online solutions, that remedied some of their problems. The amount of money and time invested was well worth the outcome, and this client continues to request reassessments from me periodically. As time has evolved, they have come to appreciate the value of these small investments. The organization has even allocated a specific budget for IT assessments and consulting that was previously not in place. And it all started with a discovery meeting.

Other Benefits of the Discovery Meeting

The discovery meeting, as part of the IT assessment, certainly provides an organic approach to investigating the information technology needs of an organization. But in addition to its obvious purpose of fact finding, the discovery meeting also has other benefits. One already mentioned includes the opportunity for executives and owners to gain an appreciation of the importance of information technology as it pertains to the goals of the organization. Key decision-makers come together to select which projects are worthy of consideration given the overall mission and direction of the business.

As availability of information has exploded over the last several decades, the natural trend has been for individuals as well as organizations to become subspecialized. As previously mentioned, this is especially true of information technology systems. Subspecialization allows greater expertise to be shared efficiently by having a select few acquire in-depth knowledge of a subject area. But while subspecialization is often advantageous, it also has some negative aspects. Failure to adequately communicate and educate others about the field in question can create boundaries between individuals and departments. When this occurs, subspecialization is less of a benefit and more of a hindrance. Tasks go uncompleted, resources become restricted, and roadblocks are developed.

Discovery meetings provide a forum in which communication and education can take place. IT managers can explain current problems and challenges to executives and owners. Owners can define in which direction the organization should be headed. Risk-versus-resource allocation can be openly discussed in accordance with business values and operations. Because of the natural complexity of information technology systems, perhaps this field requires such forums more than other subspecialized fields. If everyone can understand the issues well, then a unified solution and plan can be devised for both the short term and long term that meet the organization's goals and needs.

As an information technology consultant, I serve not only as an investigator but also as liaison. Translating technical problems and solutions into practical terms for business professionals is an important aspect of my job. I like to call this "Bridging the Gap." Business owners and executives need to know what it means for their businesses if IT disasters occur. At the same time, I must educate IT managers on the availability of resources and the degree of risk business executives are willing to take when some of the IT solutions are not chosen. At times I even serve as a coach for IT managers, teaching them better communication and soft skills in dealing with executive staff. By choosing an outside consultant to conduct an IT assessment, the organization often gains a valuable go-between who can assist in interdepartmental communications and education.

The discovery meeting as it pertains to an outside consultant also serves another valuable purpose. The content of the information being discussed during an IT assessment and discovery meeting is certainly important and privileged. Most organizations would not want to share this information with just anyone, and therefore trust between an IT consultant and an organization is crucial. A two-hour meeting can provide business representatives with a feeling about the trustworthiness of a consultant. The meeting can also provide an impression of how the consultant interacts with the staff. A particular consultant's personality, communication style, and approach may or may not be a good match for your business. For the cost of a brief discovery meeting, these impressions can help you determine whether a particular consultant is right for you in the long term.

Not long ago, I received a call from a potential client located a good distance from my office. They did not wish to pay me to come on-site for a discovery meeting as they were unsure if I was a good match for their needs. As a compromise, we conducted a series of emails and phone conferences in which a great deal of information was shared and pertinent questions asked. After a short time, the organization felt comfortable enough with my approach to arrange a formal site visit. While the lack of a face-to-face meeting initially was not ideal, the remote discovery meetings eventually led to a feeling of trust and comfort that allowed them to move forward.

Choosing the Right Person for the Job

Identity theft is a significant concern in our world of logins, passwords, and secure access. In fact, nearly 300,000 identity-theft complaints were filed in the United States alone during 2009, representing a progressive trend over the past decade[3]. Just imagine someone else having access to your most personal information. Simply by gaining access to your accounts and databases, an identity thief knows nearly everything about your life. This creates quite a feeling of vulnerability.

Now consider the process of choosing an IT consultant for your organization or business. The same logins, passwords, and security access that are taken without permission during an identity theft encounter are voluntarily handed over to a professional consultant who plans to investigate and analyze your IT system. The consultant has access to privileged information, which may include financial data, patents, research information, market analyses, and much more. Because this information is vital to your organization's success, choosing an IT consultant must be taken seriously. In other words, the consultant you select must be someone who is trustworthy in addition to being well qualified.

How do you determine if a consultant is trustworthy and qualified? Does a discovery meeting offer enough time to make this assessment? Probably not. The discovery meeting can certainly give you some insight about a person's knowledge and personality, but coming to a determination of that person's trustworthiness and performance takes time. That makes finding a good IT consultant a challenge for many organizations. Because of security concerns and privileged-information access, some businesses choose not to go outside of their own organization for periodic IT evaluations. Unfortunately, if in-house IT managers lack adequate qualifications, this choice is hardly advantageous to the organization.

As is the case with many fields of subspecialized expertise, two key sources of information help an organization choose a trustworthy and reputable consultant. The first source of information resides in a consultant's experience with various organizations. Seek a list of other organizations that have utilized the services of the consultant, and be sure to contact them if permitted. Ask detailed questions about confidentiality, performance, timeliness, communications, and professional behavior. While some organizations may be hesitant to be specific, you can usually "read between the lines" and gain a good perspective of their honest opinion of the IT professional. Sometimes you can also sign a Non-Disclosure Agreement (NDA) to gain more insight. After hearing the same positive descriptions repeatedly, you can be reassured of a consultant's professionalism and skills.

The second source of information comes directly from word-of-mouth referrals from friends, colleagues, and other respected professionals. It never hurts to ask people within your industry about qualified individuals who can serve as IT consultants. Often the same name or names will surface, and these will provide you with a solid lead in finding the right person. Unsolicited testimonials regarding IT consultants used by other organizations can certainly point you in the right direction. As an aside, good IT consultants are also usually not seeking new clients aggressively. Instead, clients are more commonly seeking them because the field is under-populated by well-qualified individuals. Finding a consultant who must schedule an appointment with you weeks ahead is often a good sign.

Unfortunately, standard qualifications and certifications within the field of information technology are far from ideal. These topics will be considered in later chapters that deal with your own IT managers and personnel. However, the number of certification exams and training programs are so numerous and varied that identifying those that are relevant to your organization is nearly impossible. A slew of alphabet-soup letters after a consultant's name may mean absolutely nothing in relation to the IT system your organization operates.

I am from a computer engineering background; I have the bias that the field of engineering offers a great foundation for being an IT consultant. Professional engineers are naturally educated in designing and constructing networks and systems. In addition, professional engineers have the ability to focus on the big picture while remaining immersed in the details. My hope is that high-level information technology curriculums will eventually require formal education in engineering programs. But until IT education becomes more standardized, reliance on experience and referrals remains the key to finding well-qualified IT consultants.

Moving Forward

The discussion regarding IT assessments in this chapter assumes that your organization has made an initial decision to examine its current IT situation. But as you are now aware, information technology is rapidly changing and thus requires examination on an ongoing basis. The initial IT assessment therefore represents a starting point for identifying issues and planning tasks to resolve any urgent problems that may exist. Subsequent assessments and meetings will then be required to ensure that tasks were completed and that any new IT issues have not surfaced. Due to the fast evolution of changes in information technology, not all the issues in your business may be internal. Ongoing IT trends and developments can create problems for your organization as well.

Generally, periodic assessments and follow-up meetings should be conducted annually at a minimum. Of course, this varies with the number and severity of problems your organization may be experiencing. An organization with a complex IT system and multiple urgent issues may require formal assessments every month until stability is achieved. In contrast, a business with well-defined IT processes in place may need reevaluations just once a year. Factors such as monetary budgets, time resources, and technical obstacles also affect how quickly tasks are completed and resolved. The important thing is to have reassessments often enough to ensure that progress is being made. The initial discovery meeting helps provide a good baseline to measure this progress.

Having covered the initial assessment, the highlights of the discovery meeting, and the selection of an outside IT consultant, our focus will now be directed toward the most important issues often identified in an organization. These so-called "urgent fixes" become an immediate focus in order to protect your organization from information loss, and understanding their importance is imperative in preventing disasters and preserving business continuity.

References
3   Identity Theft: http://www.ftc.gov/sentinel/reports/sentinel-annual-reports/sentinel-cy2009.pdf

CHAPTER 3

First Things First:
Targeting High-Priority Fixes

One afternoon, I was contacted by a law enforcement agency inquiring about my consultative services. Another client had referred me, but the agency was hesitant to explain exactly what its current dilemmas were. Whether the agency's hesitation was due to confidentiality or embarrassment, I soon found out just how serious their problem was. In short, the agency had lost three years of case-study data on various criminal investigations because of an IT system failure. Their hardware system had failed, and despite having tape backups in place, no one had bothered to ensure that the backups were actually working. Not only was the effort to recover the data going to be costly for them, but because they had multiple hard drives, the chance of full data recovery was not very likely.

In today's information world, data is extremely valuable. Can you imagine the district attorney's or the crown prosecutor's reaction upon learning that some case data had been permanently lost? The days of paper files and hard-copy storage are gone. Electronic storage is now the standard, and this change has brought about both positive and negative situations. On the up side, storage requires a fraction of the physical space it did previously, with accessing and organizing information becoming much simpler. At the same time, the consolidation of such data means that it is subject to disaster more easily should IT failures occur. This is why disaster recovery is among the most important subjects of a discovery meeting.

While the action plan devised from a discovery meeting may have many steps and require adjustments over time, the immediate steps typically involve addressing urgencies and small high-impact projects that provide the greatest mitigation of risk for the organization. Those bite-sized projects that enable effective disaster recovery and maintain business continuity are among the most important. It would hardly make sense to tackle other information technology considerations until these areas were stabilized appropriately. Once these projects are resolved, the approach to remedy other situations without disruption of operations can be determined. Some projects require simple upgrades without any disruption in continuity, while others demand major overhauls that must be well coordinated with daily activities.

Reducing immediate risk requires a preliminary survey of key IT system components, and an important purpose of the discovery meeting is to perform a high-level analysis of these areas. If problems are found, a more in-depth investigation then takes place. Ideally, projects that are quick and easy to complete are prioritized in the plan of action, but on occasion larger projects demand urgent attention because of the greater risk they represent. At each point, decisions regarding resource investments and risk tolerance must be made. Having all the decision-makers present during the discovery meeting process is therefore a significant benefit. This facilitates the efficiency with which decisions can be made and subsequently how rapidly urgent fixes are implemented.

In this chapter we will cover the standard approach to identifying areas that involve the greatest risk for an organization regarding information technology, and we will discuss the basic principles of prioritizing initial IT projects. In essence, these initial projects focus on putting out fires while maintaining a long-term perspective on the future IT needs of the organization. In doing so, risk can be reduced quickly and resources used most appropriately to accomplish the IT goals of the business.

Taking a Tour of the Data Center

The next step after the preliminary question-and-answer session in the discovery meeting involves a tour of the organization's data center. Much can be learned from a simple tour. Servers and networking hardware can be visually examined to assess a variety of things concerning good IT practices. Is all the equipment located in one area or distributed in different locales? Does the equipment have ample space and cool air to accommodate equipment heat dissipation? Are equipment fans clean, or are they congested with dust and debris? Are they running quietly or making unusually loud sounds during normal operations? Is the cabling a rat's nest, or is proper cable management in place? A site inspection of the data center is well worth your time.

On a recent data center tour involving a new client, I noticed right off the bat upon entering the room the number of amber and red blinking lights on several hard drives. I began to inquire if anyone had investigated these to determine the problem, and the young IT manager next to me apologetically said no. As it turned out, the organization had a virtualized IT system using a redundant storage system. No one had noticed that two of the hard drives had failed because other hard drives were picking up the slack. Unfortunately, the organization was operating with no available hot spares. (A hot spare is a redundant hard drive that automatically switches into operation to replace a failed drive.) One additional mishap would have created a real IT disaster.

Monitoring and alerts will be covered in detail in a later section, but many pieces of IT equipment have indicators that enable a quick visual assessment of their operational ability. If no one is paying attention to whether these indicators are green or red, then they really are serving no purpose or benefit to the organization. It only takes a few seconds in a data center to identify potential problems that may have escaped the awareness of IT personnel.

Another important question to ask when touring the data center is whether any personnel have experienced system-warning alerts or periods of equipment failure. During peak times of operations, IT systems operating at or near capacity will begin to alert system users of pending failures. These alerts may be unnoticed by IT managers unless staff has brought this information to their attention. On more than one occasion, system users have indicated that they have been receiving system alerts and slow processing speeds for weeks to months before a system failure occurred. Unfortunately, no one communicated this information to the right individuals to allow the disaster to be prevented. In addition, routine procedures for monitoring IT operations were not in place. A consultant who asks about these occurrences while touring a data center can potentially save an organization a tremendous amount of time and money in disaster-recovery costs.

Backups and Disaster Recovery

In the twenty-first century, the most valuable currency is not gold, silver, or coin…it is information. Data makes the world go 'round. Should your organization lose its precious data, the hit to its bottom line will certainly be substantial. Costs involved in recovering lost information are significant and include the value of many hours of work by IT professionals. For this reason alone, ensuring that your IT system has quality backup procedures is essential in order for you to compete and be successful. Protecting your organization's data is as important as securing its financial assets. Information is power, and those organizations that treat it as a priority will be in a position to succeed.

Addressing the location of data backup systems is one of the most important topics for any organization. Is data backed up on-site, off-site or both? Are multiple mechanisms for backups utilized, or is only one procedure in place? Who is responsible for monitoring the backup procedures and ensuring that they are functioning properly? Is information documented as part of a logging system? All of these questions are extremely important in determining if urgent fixes are needed. Having all the data stored and saved in one location places the organization's information at great risk if something disastrous happens at that location. The same risk can be there if all data is backed up off-site. Location, frequency, and monitoring of backups are core aspects of disaster-recovery planning. Backups determine disaster-recovery success perhaps more than any other areas of concern.

One of my more-unfortunate clients operated a large multi-location service organization that suffered a tremendous loss of data when its hardware system failed, and despite having IT personnel in place, no backup procedures were being conducted or monitored. As a result, the organization lost a large amount of data and requested my services in order to determine possible courses of action and how to avoid this in the future.

Trying to recover data in situations such as this is incredibly expensive and quite often disappointing. For this client, only a fraction of its data was recovered despite a significant investment of time and money. Some employees were fired as a result of this IT disaster, and many were fortunate that legal actions against them were not taken.

What do you think is the most common cause of backup failures among organizations? Interestingly, human error accounts for the majority of backup disasters. An IT staff member fails to perform scheduled tape backups, or no one checks tapes to determine if an actual backup occurred. In other cases, auto-generated backup reports have correctly identified problems where data has been improperly saved, but no one reads the reports. Therefore, their value becomes worthless except when a disaster finally strikes and responsibility for the error needs to be assigned. Like many other organizational practices, checks and balances are needed to ensure operations go as planned. Addressing how information is preserved and stored is certainly an area that requires dedicated attention.

Operational Issues

Operations when referring to IT systems is a very broad topic. But once backup strategies and procedures have been addressed, these areas are next in line when considering business continuity and prevention of disasters. The ability of an IT system to function properly depends on many working parts. Storage use, accessibility speeds, capacities, and software upgrades all influence how well (or how poorly) your organization functions day to day. Asking pertinent questions pertaining to these areas is another important part of the initial IT assessment.

Through the years, I have learned that people tend to be visually oriented when grasping conceptual ideas about IT operations. I can talk about virtualization and logical-versus-physical systems until I am blue in the face without imparting much understanding. But once I diagram a system visually, people quickly grasp the concepts. For this reason, I often make use of white boards during initial discovery meetings. I graphically illustrate the organization's current IT networks and systems for organizational leaders so that they can understand storage, servers, processing, and networking operations. The more complex a network is, the more helpful a visual demonstration becomes. And without a good understanding, it is difficult to make efficient progress.

As the initial analysis moves forward, areas of weakness in processor and storage availability, network and disk latencies, and memory usage are targeted. (Latency is a measure of time delay experienced.) Focusing on these operational areas is not only important but also offers a chance to make large impacts quickly. Oftentimes, undertaking small projects can enhance system performance immediately. Subsequently, larger projects can be planned that address the same issues over the long term. Finding priority fixes in operations allows an organization to obtain the most value for its initial investment in IT consultation. If budgets do not allow additional investments immediately, repairing urgent problems can buy the organization some time. Later, when budgets allow greater IT investments, less-urgent projects can be undertaken.

Different levels of complexity and severity dictate how these initial projects will be planned. In some cases, simple upgrades may be all that are needed to restore optimal functionality. These can often be performed without any interruption to the network or system, or they can be even scheduled during times when interference is negligible. In other cases, a more involved effort is needed. Upgrades can sometimes remedy situations in which a lack of overall capacity is hindering the function of an IT network. This may involve disk latency, CPU processing abilities, memory contention, or even network contention. (Contention is when two or more devices try to access a common resource at the same time.)

Some organizations discover during the initial portion of their IT assessment that previous IT projects were never completed properly or even implemented. Alternatively, many organizations have a mixture of technologies owing to the fact that different components were added during different periods of innovation. In both of these situations, IT rebuilds are frequently needed to enhance functionality. The strategy in implementing these rebuilds is always to minimize any disruption in continuity, so these projects are completed during downtimes (such as during a weekend) or performed in parallel to other ongoing IT projects. The speed of implementation is important, but so is the avoidance of business disruption.

Unfortunately, some organizations require more than simple upgrades or rebuilds. Some require major overhauls either because IT systems are failing, because technology is antiquated, or because initial system deployments were poorly done. The strategy of implementation is the same as smaller rebuilds in terms of efficiency and preservation of operational continuity, but often some disruption in business operations is inevitable. Decisions must be made regarding priorities and the timing of system repairs. Many factors may be involved in these decisions; having executives as well as IT managers involved in the process is important.

Documentation Issues

On a personal level, most everyone has struggled with documentation issues. All those passwords and logins required to access personal accounts must be documented somewhere secure and safe. Likewise, important communications and correspondence must be documented and organized. Some of us do this well, while most of us don't. Organizations are no different. A large part of my IT consultation services frequently addresses inadequate documentation and how information can be retrieved when it has not been properly secured.

Documentation regarding information technology involves numerous items. The location of equipment, equipment serial numbers, equipment warranties, vendor contact lists, passwords, and logins are the most obvious documentation concerns. In addition, documentation of other processes is needed. When were the systems updated last? Where is critical information stored and cataloged? Is documentation contained in hard-copy form, soft-copy form, or both? Is documentation maintained on-site, off-site, or both? You can imagine what troubles an organization may experience if these items are poorly documented and/or placed in vulnerable locations.

One project in which I participated involved a municipality that had recently undergone significant staff as well as vendor turnover. Because of this turnover, over several years the entire IT system suffered from poor documentation. As a result, neither the municipality nor the vendors could rely on various tasks to be completed on schedule. Nothing was documented, and accountability was poor. Developing procedures within the municipality's system to accomplish operational tasks was certainly a challenge due to the lack of baseline information. But after gathering staff to assist with the project, we eventually created a system that documented everything. We had cataloged all of our activities in the system, all the equipment present, each component's configuration, all passwords and logins, the system's capabilities, and any outstanding issues that remained by the time we were done. Because of proper documentation, the municipality could once again operate efficiently and meet expectations. In addition, when we were called back a year later for follow-up work, familiarizing ourselves with all the aspects of their information technology system was quick and easy.

Having proper documentation not only creates daily operational efficiency but also saves organizations time and money in the long run. Upgrades and rebuilds can be performed more quickly and thoroughly. Duplication of efforts is minimized since information is more accessible. And should a disaster occur, proper documentation helps get the system rapidly back to full capacity. Once again, investing in preventative measures such as documentation eliminates significant resource costs during a crisis. Documentation is also a means by which an organization protects its data. Remember: information is today's most valuable commodity.

Unfortunately, many IT managers take this concept of information and apply it to their own personal situations within the organization, and neglect the proper documentation of passwords and key IT system information, falsely assuming that this affords them greater job security. They withhold knowledge from their employers and thus have power to hold the organization hostage. In my experience, this assumption is wrong and can actually backfire on such individuals. Business owners and executives become nervous when documentation is poor. Instead of valuing an individual more because he or she holds key information, organizations become uneasy and concerned about such a situation, as they rightfully should. When this happens, an organization often takes action to secure its own interests, which may be to the detriment of the individual.

Organizations that are proactive in documenting their resources and databases often employ an intranet as part of their IT systems. This could be as simple as a directory on a file server where key individuals in the organization can access needed information. This may contain the location and serial number of a piece of equipment, or it could be a directory outlining various skills among staff within the organization. Such knowledge-based efforts facilitate efficiency and minimize firefighting, as crises can be handled much more readily. Assessing documentation procedures during the IT assessments should receive a higher-priority status.

Examining the IT Budget

Every department within an organization must fight for budgetary allowances. Marketing must demonstrate the applicability of industry metrics and the effectiveness of its strategies. Research and development must show how financial investments equate to eventual products and services. But while these areas of the organization have a history of consistently securing the budget resources they need, information technology does not. Because IT is a relatively new field in the grand scheme of things, many organizations view information technology as an operational expense only. In other words, paying for a file server is no different than paying the organization's utility and phone bills each month. Allocating part of the organization's budget for IT investments is often much more painful than other operational departments.

In my experience as an IT professional, 90 percent of organizations have no budgetary allowance for information technology systems. When problems arise, funds must be taken from discretionary sources since no contingency dollars exist for IT crises or repairs. Unfortunately, the amount of money spent by organizations during an IT crisis or disaster is exponentially more than the money that would have been spent on prevention and maintenance efforts. Instead of constructing a "fire-retardant" structure, the organization has chosen to put out fires one by one, as they occur. The cost in money and time is significantly more, and the productivity of the organization suffers as a result.

The lack of budgetary allocations in IT is due to other factors as well. For one, many executives lack general knowledge about the necessity of up-to-date information technology in today's global environment. Regardless of the industry, IT plays a role in all forms of commerce, and therefore an ongoing investment must be considered in order to position an organization well among its competitors. This is further compounded by the fact that changes in information technology evolve rapidly; entirely new developments and innovations occur every year, so IT systems implemented this year will likely be outdated and obsolete a few years down the road. These trends demand that some monies continually be set aside for IT development, and chief financial officers and other executives must be educated about these needs.

Another reason for a lack of an IT budget is due sometimes to the characteristics of IT managers themselves. By nature, IT professionals are detail-oriented and tend to focus primarily on technical issues. Their communication skills are often less well developed than is their technical expertise, thus it may be difficult for them to describe their needs for IT investment and the practical issues involved. Even if they have some of the necessary soft skills, their ability to "sell" the need to a CFO and secure funding may be poor. These are not skills that IT managers often acquire through their education process or job experience. But in order to fight for an IT budget amidst limited resources, these skills must be considered essential.

Securing a budgetary amount during the initial IT assessment is not necessarily a priority; however, the assessment is an opportune time to demonstrate how preventative measures could have saved an organization tremendous amounts of time and money. As urgent problems are identified during the initial discovery meeting, both short-term and long-term strategies can be discussed for immediate and future resolutions. Initiating a conversation about an annual IT budget to cover long-term projects and ongoing maintenance allows executives to be educated about the organization's IT needs. You don't want to lose a valuable opportunity to demonstrate the need for an IT budget when clear evidence for budget allocations exists.

From Crisis Mode to Maintenance Mode

After an organization has addressed the above issues, its most urgent IT problems can be identified. Backups, operations, documentation, and IT budgets compose the majority of areas that reveal potential vulnerabilities that require immediate attention. Because the main focus is to avert disasters and preserve business continuity, defining small, "bite-sized" projects that reduce risk and maintain functionality in the short term are given priority. However, once these projects are planned and completed, a shift in focus to long-term solutions needs to occur.

The discovery meeting, as previously mentioned, allows an organization to get to know an IT consultant in terms of trustworthiness and his or her ability to interact with the organization. The process of addressing urgent problems and short-term solutions enables this to occur to an even greater extent. By the time the quick fixes have been completed, an organization should have a good feel for whether a long-term relationship with a particular IT consultant is desired. Even at this juncture, the amount of resource investments is likely small and well worth it. By beginning with a discovery meeting and attending to urgent problems, an organization has the chance to make educated decisions about the level of long-term investments it wishes to make and with whom it wishes to make them.

In moving forward, a shift toward prevention and maintenance becomes important. In summary, these efforts involve three major categories of investment: the right technologies, the right tools, and the right personnel. Subsequent sections of this book will offer a detailed look at these categories that takes into consideration the fact that all of these fields are constantly changing. Regardless, understanding the importance of each and knowing which questions to ask on a regular basis will provide a clearer perspective on the IT needs of your organization.

CHAPTER 4

What's Good IT Without the Right Technology?

A friend of mine who was in sales years ago traveled a great deal as a result of his job. He was constantly on his computer, checking emails, sending sales projections, and handling a myriad of other tasks that required Internet connectivity. For months he struggled from place to place, trying to find wireless connections that would enable him to do his job well. Airports, hotels, restaurants, and cab rides would frustrate him endlessly due to a lack of connectivity. Other sales colleagues and competitors were outperforming him as a result. He eventually purchased a wireless broadband adapter for his laptop that provided him with Internet access almost anywhere. His job efficiency improved immediately and dramatically while his level of frustration dropped, and before long his sales figures were on par with everyone else. All he needed was the right technology in order to level the playing field.

The same scenario applies to organizations and companies. If an organization fails to have the right technologies, it will be handicapped in competing within its industry. This is especially true of information technology, an area in which new developments and trends seem to occur almost daily. No matter what industry is being considered, up-to-date information technologies are essential to provide a business with the best opportunities. Having the right technologies for your business, whether they are servers or networks or mobile devices, may mean the difference between your success and failure.

While each organization will require different technologies depending on several factors, staying abreast of your needs and what technologies are available requires constant attention. We will explore in this chapter the most common technology areas that should be regularly assessed. These serve as the foundations of an IT system upon which your business can excel. Ensuring availability, reliability, and scalability of the right technologies lets your organization focus on what's really important rather than constantly putting out fires.

For those of you not interested in the specific technologies available, you can skip this chapter and go to Chapter 5: Work Smarter, Not Harder: Having the Right Tools in Place.

Servers

Computer servers represent a serious investment in your IT infrastructure. File servers, email servers, and storage servers, whether combined or separate, lie at the heart of your organization's IT capabilities. Over the last few decades, the choices of different types of servers and their functions have grown. Businesses can now tailor their technological needs to the exact types of server functions they require. Without a good understanding of what server options are available, business functionality may be less than optimal.

For the sake of simplicity, you can choose from three types of servers. These options include tower servers, rack-mount servers, and blade servers. Most everyone is familiar with tower servers. These are stand-alone servers that look like an oversized computer and in reality can function as a computer as well as a server (though this is rarely necessary and highly not recommended). Each tower server has its own power supply and requires its own cabling for network connectivity. For this reason, along with its size, tower servers are best suited for small businesses that do not have tremendous IT demands. As demand increases, the amount of space these servers require as well as power and cabling make them less than ideal.

The second option is rack-mount servers. Compared to tower servers, these pizza box–shaped servers are much more compact. Because of this, several rack-mount servers can be affixed inside an equipment cabinet, thus saving a significant amount of space. Rails located within the equipment cabinet allow rack-mount servers to slide into place, like drawers in a chest, and this facilitates physical accessibility. Similar to tower servers, rack-mount servers also are stand-alone units and can function independently. As such, they have their own power supplies and network cabling. The greatest advantage for rack-mount servers is their ability to consolidate a business's server needs into a compact area. As IT demands grow, this becomes very attractive for many organizations where space is at a premium.

The most recent type of server available for organizations is the blade server. Blade servers are notably different than tower and rack-mount servers. For one, these are not stand-alone servers but require placement in a special type of chassis in order to function. The blade chassis is then installed into an equipment cabinet similar to rack-mount servers. Without the blade chassis, blade servers are useless. In fact, blade chassis are proprietary in nature and must match the blade servers that are placed inside them. For example, a Dell blade server would not work in an HP blade chassis, and vice versa. Like rack-mount servers, blade servers allow consolidation of server power in a small area, but more important, only the blade chassis must receive power and network cabling. Multiple blade servers can therefore be placed in one chassis that requires minimal cabling, and should problems arise, troubleshooting is much less complicated. This is particularly useful for large organizations that require a large number of servers.

Blade servers do have some disadvantages. For one, their operation is typically much louder due to necessary fans used to cool an increased amount of equipment in a smaller space. While density is a value, the amount of heat generated within the same amount of space with blade servers is greater, and this requires additional cooling needs. In addition, a bare blade-server chassis in a functional configuration costs significantly more than a regular rack-mount chassis. Unless you have a certain number of servers (usually eight or more), it may not be cost effective to obtain a blade-server chassis. Last, the amount of power utilized by blade servers may be more compared to regular rack-mount servers or tower-based servers. This is particularly true for organizations that have fewer numbers of servers. Organizations with numerous servers will enjoy a reduction in power costs with blade servers once they reach a certain capacity.

Virtualized Servers/Virtual Machines

The term "virtual" originates from the study of optics as it pertains to image reproduction. For instance, a mirror reproduces an image of an object, but because the image is not real and physical, it is deemed virtual. With this in mind, the concept of virtual machines (VMs) can be better understood. By applying virtualization software to a server, a separation between the server's hardware and its operational ability can be achieved. In essence, the software creates a virtual "container" in which all the files of the server are duplicated and emulated. This software container, or layer, is called a hypervisor. With this in place, multiple virtual machines can utilize a physical server's resources through the hypervisor even though each virtual machine may use a different operating system.

Traditionally, each physical server has its own IP address. A network accesses a server based on its IP configuration on the network. However, if that server becomes disabled, the network or portion of the network is inoperable until it can be repaired. In contrast, virtual machines have their own IP configurations, with each one having access to several physical servers that run the virtualization software. If one physical server becomes disabled, the virtual machines are thus still able to function normally by using the hardware and resources of other physical servers on the network. This high availability becomes an important issue in disaster-recovery situations.

The advantages of VMs clearly stem from the more efficient use of hardware resources, the elimination of underutilized redundancy in the IT system, and the ability to minimize downtime when servers malfunction. Larger organizations therefore enjoy greater advantages from such systems. As for disadvantages, indirect access of the physical server through the hypervisor is less efficient than direct access, and if multiple VMs are accessing a single physical server, variable performance may develop if workloads are high. While these issues may require specific attention, the advantages of virtual machines for large IT systems far outweigh the disadvantages.

Workstations

Over the last several years, two camps of thought have developed over how workstations should be constructed and incorporated into an IT infrastructure. One camp, which is older and focused on short-term costs, believes that workstations should be built according to the current needs of the organization at the time. In other words, a workstation selected this month may be completely different than other workstations that exist in the organization purchased only months previously. While each workstation is connected to the network and considered a clone of all the others, a new workstation may be completely different compared to other workstations depending on when it was added. Different brands and different capabilities lead to inherent mismatching of equipment, and this can create IT problems. While the investment outlay is less as workstations are added piecemeal, the eventual long-term costs in IT troubleshooting can be significantly more, comparatively.

The other school of thought calls for a standardization of workstations that allows uniform capabilities within the organization. This may cost more initially, because some workstations have functionality not needed by everyone in the organization. However, the long-term savings in repair and downtime costs make this worthwhile. Because all workstations are the same, the failure of one workstation can be easily remedied with the replacement of an identical workstation. Workstations customized and built with different capacities are often not interchangeable. Standardization ensures that all equipment will match well within the network; this will do away with the problem of having to deal with different brands or components that may create problems in communications or functionality.

In addition to these advantages, standardization of workstations often allows better support situations. If workstations are a well-known brand (such as IBM, Hewlett Packard, or Dell), 1-800 equipment support is usually available and allows rapid replacement of nonfunctioning equipment. Having standardized workstations facilitates this support further. In my experience, customization of individual workstations is typically not required for most organizations, and scrimping on initial costs is usually more expensive over time. Therefore, choosing standardized workstations as part of your IT infrastructure is often the best choice.

Incidentally, I have several clients who have adopted a "purchase cycle" for their new workstations on an annual basis. Group A gets new computers this year, group B the next year, and group C the subsequent year. Everyone as a result gets a new system every three years, and all the workstations within the network are relatively new. This has benefits in terms of warranty coverage and vendor support, and the organization enjoys a planned expenditure schedule for replacement of 33 percent annually. This practice makes things more manageable, keeps the IT system current, helps stabilize corporate cash flow and budgets, and minimizes workstation variability within the IT infrastructure.

Printers

When considering printers for your information technology infrastructure, you have to consider a variety of features. Printers come in all shapes, sizes, and capacities. For example, you can choose inkjet or laserjet printers. Some printers within the organization may be black and white, while others are color. A printer also may be located on the network for several users to access or could simply be a printer shared on a single computer. Even the consumables used by different printers can be pertinent because paper, cartridges, and other supplies can account for significant operational expenses. These aspects must be considered for each and every printer within the organization in order to effectively allocate printing resources.

One of the most important considerations regarding printers is the printer load. Determining the print load per week or per month on a given printer can determine a printer's required capacity. If users are waiting prolonged amounts of time for documents to print, then the capacity should be increased to accommodate peak loads. This information often helps you determine if a printer should be shared on a network or simply available from a given computer.

Printers can have multipurpose functions as well. Larger printers may have capacities for copying, faxing, and scanning in addition to printing. However, multimodality functioning may not be needed throughout the organization. Determining which printers should offer unimodality versus multimodality function is therefore essential in order to minimize costs and provide smooth operations.

The final aspect in selecting printers for your IT system involves security issues. Documents that contain confidential information or privileged data should not be printed in public areas within the organization. For example, the accounting department and the CFO may need a dedicated printer for their printing needs. Human resources and research and development may have similar needs. Failing to consider privacy aspects in certain departments ahead of time may result in duplication of costs when printers have to be reconfigured or relocated. Asking these questions ahead of time can help an organization develop an ideal printing system without suffering unnecessary expenses.

Network Switches

In the consideration of the components of information technologies for your organization, we have already discussed workstations, servers, and networks. Each workstation must connect to a server or possibly multiple servers, and these connections are what define the IT network. However, other components exist in between these connections that enable proper functioning. As the cable leaves a workstation, it travels to a server as its ultimate destination. But in between are network switches, routers, and firewalls that serve other purposes. In this section we will consider having the right switch technologies as part of your IT system.

Suppose you live in the suburbs outside a metropolitan city. In order to earn a living, you must travel to work every morning along with many other commuters and then return home every evening. As you drive from residential streets to two-lane highways to four-lane highways to major freeways and then back, the volume of traffic increases or decreases steadily. The size, or capacity, of the roadways must accommodate peak traffic in order to avoid delays. When considering an IT network, the same considerations apply. As network pathways come closer to destination servers, "wider" network cables are needed to accommodate the increase in traffic. Workstation, laptop, printer, and PC users converge from different locales onto common cables as they approach the actual servers.

Switches are components along these routes and essentially serve as traffic lights or traffic cops that make sure everyone has a turn to access the server. Information can move from the server to the user or vice versa, but switches ultimately determine access to and from. Some switches are considered "dumb" because they cannot be manipulated or provide useful statistical data about themselves. This would be analogous to a four-way stop sign at an intersection. Traffic is still managed; each car comes to a temporary halt, but no information about the traffic patterns is gained. In contrast, manageable switches provide information about different aspects of network traffic. This information may include flow diagnostics, performance ability, peak usage times, and more. They provide "visibility" to the network. Manageable switches in our traffic analogy would be comparable to traffic lights with sensors that change in response to the presence of vehicles on the road. These active devices allow traffic information to be used to augment the overall system.

When you consider the right technology for your organization, consider manageable switches as clearly the most useful. In a well-designed network, the infrastructure should always be constructed to accommodate peak usage rather than average usage among users. Manageable switches allow an organization to better determine when and what peak usage may be in addition to the location of the greatest congestion of traffic. With this information, more-efficient networks can be constructed to enhance overall performance and efficiency. Even though the cost of a manageable switch is more than that for an unmanageable "dumb" one, the amount of data obtained from your network is well worth the additional investment.

Routers

If switches are the traffic lights within networks for users to access servers, then routers are the traffic lights permitting flow and access among different networks. In other words, routers are active devices that allow internetworking to occur. The basic building blocks of the Internet are in reality millions of interconnected networks, with routers being the devices that control the rules by which these networks communicate. In order for one network to communicate with another, routers must verify that each network abides by the established rules. If so, internetworking is allowed.

Firewalls are types of routers with established rules for internetworking that typically allow free outgoing access to other networks but limit or block incoming traffic. In situations in which organizations wish to allow to-and-from access between different networks, routers can have specific rules to enable this communication. Usually in this instance, firewalls are added as a component for additional security; this will be discussed in the next section.

For an organization considering the right technology as it pertains to routers, adequate capacity is a key feature. Ensuring that a router allows adequate traffic between networks to accommodate the organization's needs is important. Additionally, different routers have different abilities. For example, an organization may choose to have a router that allows access to more than one Internet service provider (ISP). Because a single ISP is not functional 100 percent of the time, having a router that has multiple wide area network (WAN) ports enables connection to another ISP for functional backup security. In this situation, a router is chosen that allows redundancy and better reliability for the organization to operate seamlessly.

Not long ago (ca. 1998), more than 90 percent of all Internet backbone routers operated on a platform built by Cisco. (Backbone refers to the main data routes between large interconnected networks and core routers in the Internet often called tier 1 networks.) Competition has reduced this statistic over time, though Cisco's portion is still significant. Consider this, since choosing a router with which your IT staff is familiar is important. As will be discussed later about having the right IT personnel, their certifications in such technologies can provide some safeguards should troubles arise. Choosing a router that meets all the organization's needs but is poorly understood by the IT staff can erase all the benefits it may provide. A router that provides the proper capacity and ability for the business and is familiar to your staff is important when making a router selection.

Firewalls

Firewalls represent a layer above routers that offer additional protection and also control access between networks. While firewalls were not quite as comprehensive in the past, today's firewalls offer a multitude of features. In choosing the right firewall technology, obtaining features that best serve your organization is important. Educating yourself about the different features available is helpful in making this selection.

One fairly recent feature added to firewalls is the ability to conduct web filtering, which can block specific content from the web while allowing other content to pass through into your network. For example, web sites identified as inappropriate, such as those containing pornography, gambling, or hate-related content, can be selectively blocked by firewalls as desired. As is the case with virus-protection software, firewall subscription services can categorize various web content and offer category groups that can then be blocked. These subscriptions services are frequently updated just like virus protection services are. Similarly, instant messaging, social networking sites, and other communications can be selectively blocked by some firewalls.

One of the other assets a firewall can provide is the ability to allow secure remote network connections. Virtual private networks, VPNs, are facets of some firewalls that enable users or other networks to connect to a central network over the Internet. By encrypting the connection, a VPN provides a secure and safe connection between the user and the network despite the connection traversing the Internet, which is clearly a public environment. In some cases, special software must be loaded onto both the network and remote users' computer in order to utilize a VPN. More recently, special types of VPNs (called SSL-VPNs) initiate this connection by using a web browser without the need of such software.

Firewalls have changed a great deal in recent years, and further changes are likely to evolve in the near future. In choosing a firewall for your IT system, what specific features you want is the most important decision, followed by making sure that the firewall you choose allows frequent updating. In addition, since multiple vendors are available, choosing one with a proven history of quality, performance, and support is preferable.

Networks

Having talked about switches, routers, and workstations, discussing networks within the IT system is the next logical step. Networks are essentially configured in two different fashions. Traditional (physical) local area networks (LANs) describe networks that require physical proximity between workstations, hubs, switches, and routers because one-to-one relationships exist between these components. In other words, each component must plug into the network through cabling and traverse different components of the network to reach the server. This type of system obviously has limitations, particularly for large organizations or organizations demanding secure or remote-network access. As a result, most physical networks exist in smaller organizations.

In contrast to physical LANs, virtual local area networks (VLANs) allow the creation of logical networks that surpass the physical constraints of traditional LANs. Instead of one-to-one relationships between the physical components of a network, multiple networks can utilize physical structures and create numerous VLANs. For example, suppose a group of users in an organization operated on a single physical LAN. Accounting department users worked in the same network as research and development users. As information was sent from one user through the network, everyone else on that network could have access to that information. In order to separate user groups, different physical LANs would have to be created. This would duplicate the amount of physical hardware needed and require the use of routers to allow communication between networks.

VLANs offer a better solution to this situation. Instead of information from one network having to travel along one IT pathway, numerous networks can share the same pathway and hardware. Multiple VLANs can be established that allow only the users associated with a particular VLAN to send and receive information specific to that network. How is this accomplished? Interestingly, network switches, known as VLAN-aware switches, are able to apply VLAN tags to data packets as they traverse the switch. These tags thus associate the information with a specific VLAN in the system. The switches and routers know which network the data packet belongs to because each information packet will have a tag indicating the VLAN.

From a performance standpoint, VLANs are much better than traditional networks because VLAN-aware switches are much faster at tossing packets around than are routers. We call this layer 3 switching. In traditional LANs, routers must direct information to different networks, and this takes comparatively longer. Additionally, VLANs reduce the amount of cables, routers, workstations, and switches needed to accomplish the same abilities compared to a typical physical routed network. Last, VLANs can enable greater security by more easily facilitating specific networks for specific users.

Storage

Data storage is another important consideration in the assessment of an organization's technology needs. Traditionally, information is stored on a computer's hard drive or on a server's hard drive. As data accumulates, storage may reach capacity and thus affect the performance of the entire IT system. As larger organizations have come to experience these difficulties, innovative solutions have allowed more-efficient ways to store data. Storage area networks (SANs) are creative alternatives to augmenting hard drives on existing devices, purchasing new devices, or creating separate physical storage areas.

SANs are single-purpose devices used only for data storage across all the networks of the IT system. The best way to envision these devices is as gigantic file servers that are massive enough to contain all the files on all your organization's hard drives. As a centralized device, all the network servers have access to the SAN.

The SAN is in essence a large storage container housing large data files that are all the files on all the hard drives of every server on the network. As a result, the SAN's aggregation of hard drives must be significantly larger with much greater capacity compared to a traditional server. Most SANs consists of a basic shelf that has numerous banks of hard drives located within that shelf. Smaller SANs may have only sixteen hard drive bays, but larger organizations may require hundreds. In any case, typical common denominators for the number of SAN hard drives present are usually between twelve to sixteen.

SANs are continuously accessing and writing files located on all the network server hard drives. As a result, SANs require 100 percent uptime as well as a dedicated access path to and from these servers. In fact, the processing capacity of the entire IT system is significantly affected by the SAN processing needs. But in turn, several advantages make SANs well worth their while for larger IT systems.

Advantages for storage area networks fall into four main categories: enhanced efficiency of operations, easier expandability, improved performance, and greater reliability. Enhanced efficiency occurs because a lesser amount of wasted hard drive space exists on the entire network. While one server may have its hard drive at capacity, three others may have unused hard drive space. Because all servers have access to the SAN and vice versa, wasted space is minimized across all servers. IT resources are thus used more efficiently, and this can effectively streamline the organization.

Second, expandability is achieved more easily and for less cost. Suppose all the servers are operating near storage capacity. Instead of having to add increased hard drive functionality to each individual server, which would be quite costly, a single additional hard drive can be added to the SAN for all servers to access. All the servers' capacities here have been increased for a fraction of the cost of a physical system.

While expandability and efficiency increase overall performance, SANs also enhance functionality simply by the number of hard drives now accessible. The speed with which operations and functions (reads and writes) can be performed is increased because servers have access to many more hard drives to access the required data. Operations are not bogged down on a single hard drive. Avoiding such delays and interruptions creates optimal performance for the IT system and the organization.

Last, SANs allow increased reliability for the entire IT system. The redundant hard drives that can be added to the network provide a greater degree of protection from component failures. By having additional redundant storage space and operational hard drives added to a network, no interruption in server functionality is experienced. Interruptions are often the case when a single server on a physical network requires the addition of drives for additional storage or redundancy. The extra cost of adding this to each individual server on a physical network is often significant.

Having a Solid Foundation

Establishing a strong information technology foundation by obtaining the correct technologies can facilitate many facets of your business. Information is accessed more easily and efficiently. Communications flow more rapidly and without interruptions. Growth and progress advance steadily because time and resources are not wasted on daily emergencies. And of course profitability is maximized in the long run as investments in the proper IT resources reduce unnecessary expenses year after year. In contrast, failing to pay attention to your organization's IT needs can result in limitations and problems that negatively affect all of these areas.

For the most part, the areas covered in this chapter focused on the basic technologies involved in creating a strong informational network within your organization. Workstations, servers, switches, routers, and firewalls are the key components of a functional network, and each of these components requires thoughtful decisions in selecting for your business. Spending time and energy as well as money to identify these needs is a wise choice. Once this has been addressed, the next step is to identify additional IT tools that can further enhance your system, allowing it to be streamlined and efficient. Data backup systems, archiving procedures, logging and ticketing, cooling and power options, and monitoring devices are among the many tools that further augment your IT system.

These tools, while not directly part of the network configuration, do allow your IT system to maximize your business's ability to achieve success. They can reduce the risk of downtime, equipment wear and tear, and unnecessary system failures. At the same time they can provide insurance against data loss in the event of a catastrophe. Dealing with some of these hardware solutions helps address risk management by implementing better redundancy and reliability but is focused on a shorter-term perspective. In the next section we will see that choosing the right IT tools requires taking a long-range look at your organization and making choices about smart risk-reduction implementations.

CHAPTER 5

Work Smarter, Not Harder: Having the Right Tools in Place

L ast year, a friend of mine decided to remodel his basement. He carefully devised a step-by-step plan that organized the sequence by which projects would be done. He arranged necessary contractors accordingly, but the majority of the work he was going to perform on his own. Everything seemed to be planned to perfection. During the first week, he began removing carpeting from the floor. He never imagined the amount of staples, nails, and glue attaching the carpet to the hardwood flooring. Equipped with a crowbar and a hand sander, my friend methodically started removing the carpet and adhesives from the floor. After a couple of weekends he was only about a third of the way done. He gave up and hired a flooring contractor to finish the job.

In about two hours, the flooring contractor accomplished what had taken my friend two weekends to do. Special nail-pullers, industrial sanders, and chemical solvents allowed the contractor to rapidly remove the carpet and leave the underlying flooring free of debris. My friend had devised the proper sequence of events and plans for remodeling but lacked the tools necessary to perform the job efficiently. Similarly, many organizations have great technologies and IT infrastructure but lack the specific tools that optimize their efficient use and maintenance. In this section we will cover some of those tools that allow an organization to operate smarter and more efficiently.

Understanding these tools before things go awry can save you a good deal of frustration and headaches.

Backup and Archiving Tools

For many organizations, the distinction between a data backup and a data archive is not well understood. These two IT tools are often lumped together in the same category. But in reality, backups and archiving represent two very different aspects of data storage and serve different purposes. Backups create duplicate replicas of server data. If data is lost and disaster recovery is needed, backups provide data files from which restoration can be performed. In contrast, archiving takes a single instance of data at a particular time and removes it to a storage system. While backups support IT operations in the event of a disaster, archiving serves an administrative function, allowing data to be stored, indexed, and retrieved when needed.

Backups are categorized according to the amount of data copied and include full backups, differential backups, and selective backups. Full-data backups copy everything on the server so that if an IT disaster strikes, copies of all files are available for easy restoration. In contrast, differential backups copy only changes in files that have been altered since the last backup was completed. This reduces the amount of work the system must perform yet still captures key changes on an ongoing basis.

Last, selective backups target only certain files for backup. Often, selective files are chosen because of limited time or capacity in backup abilities. Depending on the size of an organization, the amount of data to be copied, the capacity of the IT system, and the risk an organization is willing to take, different backup types may be chosen. The most common backup scenario is to perform full backups weekly and monthly and to perform differential backups daily. This often appeals to organizations in terms of balancing the amount of risk with which they are comfortable and the demands on the IT infrastructure.

Data backups do utilize IT storage capacity whether they are performed on-site or off-site. Multiple copies of backups may also exist in storage areas depending on the IT capacity and preferences of the organization. By having multiple copies of data files, problems with file corruption can be addressed during IT disaster management. For example, if a data file is corrupt, and this corrupt file is part of the most recent backup, an older backup file would be needed for restoration of the system. By choosing a backup file that does not contain corrupt data, system recovery is made possible without difficulty. At some point, older files are overwritten with new backup information since capacity will eventually limit the number of backup files being stored at one time. For this reason, backup files are considered short-retention files lasting days, weeks, or rarely months in duration before they are replaced.

From my perspective, backups should never be stored on a single medium or at a single site. Multiple media for storage should be used, with on-site and off-site storage being a must. This distribution of backups ensures that a single catastrophe in one location or in one medium does not wipe out your backup files and your operations at the same time. Regular assessments of your backup system are also essential to verify that the system is doing what it is supposed to do. Too often, organizations think they are performing backups when in actuality nothing is being captured. Unfortunately, many realize this after it is too late.

As a favor I performed an IT assessment for one of my relative's companies a few years back. He and his staff had been complaining of performance issues within their IT system. Within an hour, I discovered a significant other problem. The tapes that stored their backup files were completely full, and the backup system was also malfunctioning. The staff had continued to swap out the tapes every day in order to perform a new backup, but no new files were being copied. Their last working backup was over nine months old! Can you imagine if the system had crashed and nine months of data had been lost?

After replacing the existing server, I recommended both on-site and off-site backups through a couple of different types of media. In addition, automated backups as well as weekly checks of the backup system by a designated IT person were put into place. Processing speeds improved, and productivity increased immediately. My relative was fortunate that we had caught the problem before disaster struck.

In contrast to backups, archiving represents a single instance of data captured at a moment in time and stored elsewhere. Archive files are not overwritten as are backup files; instead, they are indexed and cataloged for future retrieval as needed. For example, if an email assessment of a disgruntled employee needs to be performed for legal purposes, archives provide data that can be searched. Unlike backups, archives are also kept for long periods of time. The length of time may be dictated by industry regulations in some situations, or it may be defined by the amount of risk an organization is willing to take.

The other decision regarding archiving is how often an archive file should be taken. Are daily archives needed because data is changing so frequently, or are weekly or monthly archives adequate for the retrieval needs of the organization? This can be a challenging decision, especially if legal risks in human resources and other departments are being considered. Likewise, if an archive file is corrupted, the next archive performed (or the previous one) is the next source of information. If frequency between archives is significant, data may be absent and lost on other existing archives.

The final consideration regarding backups and archiving is where to store the files and how often storage should be taken off-site. Storage Area Networks (SANs), as discussed previously, offer ideal solutions for storage of backup files. Off-site SANs provide even greater protection. For instance, if a SAN at a remote location replicates all data, and the same SAN has access to remote servers, an organization's IT system can be back up and running even when the primary site is completely down. Because the most recent backup file provides all the data needed for operations and additional servers are available, the organization can continue business as usual while the problems at the primary site are being addressed.

Whether a SAN is available or not, backups and archives should be stored at more than one location and onto different types of media (tapes, optical discs, external hard drives, e-warehouses). This process ensures redundancy and provides greater protection in the event of a disaster or should data retrieval be needed.

Cooling and Power Needs

I have consulted with many organizations that have completely ignored the basic power and cooling needs of their IT systems. They assume that with a basic electrical power supply, surge protector, and the internal equipment fans, their information technology equipment has all it needs to operate well. Unfortunately this is often not the case, especially when larger IT systems are in place.

Backup power is best supplied through batteries and/or generators. Uninterruptible Power Supply (UPS) batteries provide temporary power when primary electrical power is lost. When you consider a UPS battery supply, an important piece of information is the total equipment load being placed on the battery. As the number of devices plugged into a UPS increases, so does the total load. And as the load increases, the run time decreases, since greater power is being consumed. Therefore, battery systems with high loads may not allow adequate power while alternative power systems (such as generators) become functional. Fortunately, many UPS batteries are expandable and allow run times to be improved by adding more batteries to the UPS. It is therefore important to assess both load and required run times when assessing backup power needs.

UPS can be used to maintain power to electrical breakers in addition to providing backup power. By placing larger, integrated UPS batteries in between the primary electrical supply and electrical breakers, the entire IT system can be maintained for a period of time even if a complete primary electrical failure occurs. While isolated UPS batteries may work well for small organizations, these larger, integrated UPS systems are of greater value for large data centers running multiple servers. In addition, UPS systems provide line conditioning, which prevents surges and inconsistencies in the flow of electricity. Blips in the electrical current known as "brown-outs" cause deterioration of equipment components, and clean, consistent power is desirable for better equipment longevity.

The other major types of backup power are generators. Generators may be diesel-based or gas-based, and often these devices require a period of time to warm up before being fully operational. During this window of time, UPS battery supply is used to bridge the gap. Because generators require fuel, refueling these backup power sources is a priority. Organizations should have a contractual arrangement with a fuel service for their power generators, and also alternative fuel companies should be available in case one company is unavailable. In addition, generators should receive at minimum annual tests to ensure functionality, and fuel should be replaced periodically in order to prevent it from becoming stale.

Another important factor to consider is whether a generator requires an operator to manually switch power from the electrical grid over to a generator. Waiting for an operator to convert power over to the generator may demand longer run times for UPS batteries, and if load is a concern, automated switches may be preferred. Automated transfer switches convert to generator power once primary power failures are detected, thus saving time and human resources.

For most large IT systems, redundant power supplies are provided to servers and even larger networks. Most equipment today comes with dual power ports where different power sources can provide power to a machine. Primary and secondary power sources can be labeled by color (such as red and blue) and can provide alternate power supplies for the purpose of redundancy. In this way, if the red primary power input fails, the secondary blue power input takes over, providing seamless continuity. This concept has been applied not only to power needs but to entire networks as well.

Of course, with power comes heat. In fact, most of the input power to servers and some other IT equipment is converted to heat, which must be dissipated or cooled to prevent component damage. Additionally, the increased demand for greater-density servers with more computing power in a smaller space complicates matters further. Greater density creates greater exhaust, which raises temperatures when confined to dense spaces. IT managers can no longer rely on ambient room temperature to provide enough air flow to offset these temperature effects.

I have lost count of how many times I have walked into a small organization and found all its server components stashed away in a small office closet with the door shut. Even if the door has a vented grate, the confined space is too small to allow adequate cooling. As a result, the longevity of the equipment deteriorates, and replacement costs increase. Even in larger organizations with greater space allocations for their IT equipment, cooling needs are often neglected. Some HVAC systems shut off at night or on weekends while IT servers and networks continue to operate full time. As a result, equipment temperatures exceed the cooling ability of internal fans and ambient air flow, again resulting in overheating. In the end, the results are the same: reduced equipment longevity, impaired performance, and increased replacement costs.

For any IT system that operates multiple high-density servers, external cooling systems are a must. The amount of savings this will provide in the long run in avoiding equipment repairs and replacements is noteworthy. As a benefit, better performance of the equipment will be maintained for longer periods of time, and this will increase productivity and minimize downtimes. As IT components and servers continue to push the limits of size, speed, and space, greater attention to cooling systems will be unavoidable.

Monitoring and Alerting

An ounce of prevention is worth a pound of cure. In many areas of life today, we have come to realize that preventative efforts can save an enormous amount of time and expense in the long run. Routine oil and filter changes help preserve your car's engine. Monitoring blood pressure and lab work annually can help you identify health problems earlier, allowing disease prevention. Weatherproofing your home periodically can reduce your utility costs and the need for repairs. In each case, proactive steps are taken to ensure that your car, your body, or your home is well maintained and that problems can be avoided.

The key word here is "proactive." Rather than being reactive once a problem has already occurred, the above shows how proactive processes are put into place to reduce complications. For IT systems, similar proactive mechanisms are utilized for the same purpose. Monitoring systems and alerts are means by which the health of the IT system is assessed on a regular basis. If a potential for future problems is identified, notifications can be sent and/or actions can be taken to reduce or eliminate the condition. In essence, monitoring systems are automated processes that watch over your network and provide alerts to responsible personnel when needed.

Monitoring systems can assess a variety of processes within an IT system, including the quality of Internet connectivity, the function of application servers, the temperature environment of server components, and the amount of file-storage space. If a defined level of concern is reached, the monitoring system then signals an alert to be sent accordingly. Or in some cases the monitoring system simply reacts by taking corrective actions.

While internal monitors within a network are most common, external monitors also exist. By definition, these are outside of the organization's IT network but routinely monitor the operation of the system through Internet connections or web site functionality. If the entire IT system becomes nonfunctional, the internal monitor may no longer be operational. However, the external monitor would continue to identify a problem and send alerts accordingly. As you can see, redundancy is a common theme when putting best IT practices into place, and having both internal and external monitoring systems is another example of this. Additionally, I generally recommend a monitor to monitor the monitoring system. If the monitoring system fails without any notification, much-larger problems could ultimately occur as a result. Having a watchdog watch the watchdog can avoid this scenario.

As far as alerts are concerned, various methods are used to communicate a problem to the right personnel. Email messages are by far the most common method. But what happens if an alert stating that the email server is down is sent to the IT manager via email? Obviously the message will never be received. If this is on a weekend, it could well be Monday morning before the problem is realized. By then, employees, customers, and vendors may have become frustrated. When you consider how alerts will be sent, give some thought to the method of alerting. Text messages, voicemails, and emails are some of the options available. In addition, logs can be captured when alerts are sent, allowing a record to be kept for the organization. (Logging and ticketing will be covered in later sections.)

While alert notifications to individuals are most common, automated reactions to system alerts are certainly advantageous and skip the need for delayed human involvement. For instance, if a server determines that it is suddenly operating on backup battery power, it can generate an alert while it automatically begins performing a full-system backup. In the meantime, the battery system that has been activated has automatically switched on the power generator to begin warming up. This not only preserves continuity of function but also prevents customer dissatisfaction and shows good business sense.

Some organizations take this a step further and have alerting systems that automatically notify all organizational staff when a system is not operating correctly. This in turn avoids a barrage of emails and phone calls about the problem. By having automated response communications through system alerts, the organization is inherently more effective and efficient.

You can program different levels of severity when devising alerts and establishing monitoring parameters. Levels can be defined as simply a warning or can be labeled as critical. Each company and organization will have different thresholds for this. Regardless, having such tools in place is extremely helpful in allowing proper operations to run smoothly.

Logging

Logging is a means by which information is tagged and collected for specific purposes. For example, alerts from a monitoring system can be logged to assess patterns and frequency of problems, or perhaps emails are logged for liability protection. In short, logs are pieces of information that are collected and filed for future reference if needed. They can be used for a variety of purposes, ranging from documentation to diagnostics. The two most important questions an organization should ask about logging are what level of detail should be included in a log and how often should logs be collected. These answers will vary considerably depending on the specific organization.

From my experience, upper-level management must be involved in deciding the timing and extent of information logging. For example, some organizations may choose to log only the date and time of email correspondences rather than the entire content of the message. Other organizations that have legal concerns of liability risk or compliance may opt to log the entire email message. Once a log is created, how long should it be kept? If liability is a concern, a fairly lengthy period of time may be defined for keeping logs. Logs may also be archived in order for easy indexing and retrieval. While most logs are in text format and can be compressed easily, logs still utilize disk space. Therefore, the level of logging details and duration they should be kept must be addressed up-front.

Besides playing a role in documentation, logging also helps establish trends and patterns in an organization. For instance, if logs demonstrate that power-failure alerts repeatedly occur at three o'clock in the morning when housekeeping is running vacuum cleaners, electrical-capacity issues can be addressed so that problems are avoided. Additionally, logs of the amount of disk space used each week by network servers can be recorded; this in turn will allow the organization to predict when disk-space capacity will be reached. Using logs in this fashion can provide information that helps solve problems earlier rather than later and aid in decision-making.

Last, logging also provides a degree of accountability. Logs can record when users log in and out of a system, the specific files that were accessed, the length of time files were open, and many other user-related aspects. This can help with issues of security, task responsibility, and user-related problems that may otherwise be difficult to identify and record. Even IT staff can be monitored through logs to determine if proper maintenance and diagnostic procedures are being performed in a timely manner. While logging has many possible benefits, its specific benefits for an organization must be defined so resources can be used appropriately and not in excess.

Ticketing / Knowledge-Base

As a knowledge-base tool and a tool to make informational technologies achieve maximum effectiveness for an organization, ticketing systems are exceptional. Essentially, a ticketing system is the "help desk" system of an organization. Staff, customers, and vendors can contact the help resources of an organization and make a request. The request may be that a piece of equipment is not working properly, that software may need to be added to a system, or a variety of other complaints. Once a request is received, a ticket is created that details the information of the request. From that point forward, everything that has to do with that case or ticket is documented under its own location.

If ticketing systems are implemented effectively, a tremendous amount of information can be gained. For example, suppose staff members complain that a network printer was failing to respond to their computers. By examining a ticketing system log, a report may show that several other users reported the same problem over a period of time. Or perhaps the same user had the same difficulty six months ago. Ticketing systems allows an organization to quantify the number of times a problem has occurred, patterns of problems, problem complexity, resolution efficiency, and many other trends and data. Management reports from the system can thus be used to make informed decisions about operations and personnel.

From a user standpoint, ticketing systems allow a means by which resolution progress is being made. Tickets can also be assigned to individuals so that users know who is responsible for helping them with their requests or complaints. Notes can be added to tickets detailing past communications and actions, providing even greater information, and past tickets can be searched for similar requests or complaints, facilitating faster resolutions. All in all, ticketing systems increase efficiency of an organization and naturally create a knowledge base for the organization. If a problem exists, searching a ticket database for past remedies saves significant time and resources.

From an informational technology perspective, a healthy IT department thrives on a good knowledge base. Younger IT professionals can learn effective processes more efficiently when comprehensive knowledge resources are available. From my experience, executives also feel more comfortable when accessible knowledge resources are available to the entire organization rather than being hoarded by a few select experts. Ticketing is an excellent means by which knowledge resources can be organized and made more accessible, thus creating a knowledge base.

Knowledge bases can take many other forms such as intranets, wikis, searchable document management systems, and other collaborative systems.

Using the Toolbox

Having the correct informational technologies is not always enough to be competitive in a tough business environment. Having the correct tools to help technologies perform at their peak is equally important in today's business environment. Whether you are addressing power needs or a logging system, every tool serves a purpose and plays a role in contributing to performance. Failing to appreciate this fact will only place an organization at risk over the long run.

Like a contractor's tool box, an array of tools are available that augment different parts of your IT system. Backups and archives address file and data storage. Power and cooling needs provide stable platforms for operational continuity. Monitoring and alerts help warn of pending problems. Logging allows documentation and trend identification. Ticketing helps with organizational efficiency and knowledge collection. Making yourself aware of the benefits of each can place your organization head and shoulders above other organizations.

In my experience, too many organizations neglect these seemingly minor areas of information technology until major problems surface. By then, the problems have blossomed into greater issues that require much-larger investments in time, energy, and other resources. The key here is to be proactive and to devise a system that considers risks and concerns while promoting optimal functionality. Having a good IT system in place not only depends on networks and its components, it also depends upon the basic tools to keep it running well.

CHAPTER 6

The Right People— Assembling a Great IT Team

O ver the last few decades, the rising costs of healthcare in the United States and Canada have demanded some type of reform. Managed care has driven down reimbursement for physicians and hospitals, and these entities have found it hard to maintain profitability using the same age-old paradigms. As a result, other professionals, known as physician extenders, have entered the picture. Patients are now seen by professionals such as nurse practitioners and physician assistants rather than actual doctors for minor medical problems. Over time, the use of such individuals has been found to be beneficial for health problems that are fairly straightforward and routine. But as problems become more complex, fully trained physicians and specialists are required in order to provide quality healthcare.

The same thing has occurred in the information technology field. Smaller companies and organizations have often found that an individual with basic IT knowledge can serve as an IT manager much of the time. But as an organization's IT needs expand, growing demands for IT skills and abilities might be poorly met as neither training nor experience are adequate to accommodate needs. This problem is becoming commonplace today as the complexities of IT networks and systems require advancing knowledge and skills increases. However, unlike the medical profession, a universally accepted training and educational standard has yet to be defined.

Having the right technologies and the right tools is necessary in order to compete in today's business environment locally and globally. But without the right personnel who know how to get the most out of an IT system, problems will arise, and performance will be substandard. Navigating the maze of different training options and certifications can be confusing, to say the least. In this chapter we will consider the current climate of IT training and education to help you assess your IT needs with greater confidence. Ultimately, having the right IT professionals will provide your organization with the final piece of the puzzle to get the most out of your information technology system.

Today's IT Training Environment

The field of information technology is a relatively new field of study, but the scope of knowledge and skills that it covers is quite broad. Colleges and universities have developed curriculums that address various information-related fields such as information security, information science, and information technology, but to date, very few standards that define comprehensive expertise in the field have been developed. Information technology differs from other professions such as law, medicine, and engineering in this way.

Essentially, two camps of IT training exist. The first camp relies more heavily on the practical applications of information technology. These hands-on curriculums often consist of short one-to-two year crash courses or boot camps during which individuals learn basic applications of IT tools and technologies. Many times these training programs are vendor-specific. For example, a person may spend a year training to become certified in Microsoft technologies but have little if any exposure to other types of IT systems, networks, or components. If this person is then placed in a management position over an organization's IT department, a good chance exists that his or her skills may be inadequate to meet the organization's needs.

The other training option is more traditional. Certain four-year college degrees cover different aspects of information management and technology. Again, a defined curriculum is not standardized among different types of institutions, and these programs tend to focus on theoretical concepts regarding IT systems and management. Despite having a good foundation of IT knowledge, these programs are limited when it comes to imparting practical skills. Graduates of these programs often acquire management positions in IT departments but lack the working knowledge necessary to make sound decisions and to fully contribute to the problem-solving needs. A competent IT manager has a full complement of theoretical knowledge and solid practical skills. Unfortunately, these professionals are hard to find.

From my perspective, the problem stems from not having better standardization within the industry. Training is not being performed well because too many training centers and colleges approach education and skill instruction from different perspectives. Most tend to focus on a narrow aspect of training rather than encompassing a broad curriculum that addresses the larger field of information management. For example, someone may be trained in IT networking and web servers but have no real understanding of virtualization techniques. As a result, trained IT professionals can see the trees around them but fail to envision the entire IT forest.

Ongoing study is also mandatory for your IT professional to be relevant in today's business climate. Technologies are changing so rapidly that continuing education, whether gained through industry journals, periodic courses, or organized seminars, is a must. Without this, knowledge as well as skills can quickly become outdated.

The best-qualified information technology experts approach IT from an engineering perspective. Building IT networks and orchestrating IT systems is very similar to building bridges and other complex engineering feats. Engineering teaches individuals to focus not only on minute details but also on the association between these details and the bigger picture. Though an IT system may not be as tangible as the Golden Gate Bridge in San Francisco, the same methodologies of design are quite similar. In addition, well-recognized engineering programs teach individuals not only knowledge but also good problem-solving skills that translate into successful practical applications in the real world. Once an individual has gained an ability to understand and apply different algorithms and procedures to different situations, future IT demands can be handled more easily.

The other reason I say that engineering is an ideal discipline for IT skills training is its ability to combine theoretical and practical education. I attended the University of Alberta and obtained a four-year degree in engineering. While technically part of the electrical engineering program, I took all my electives in computing sciences. As a result, I was awarded a degree in computer engineering. However, before I could apply for an engineering license, I had to complete a minimum of another four years of apprenticeship under a licensed engineer's supervision or mentorship. After investing this time as an engineer in training (EIT), I gained a comprehensive set of skills and knowledge and was awarded my professional engineering status.

The key to choosing an IT professional for your organization is to search for someone with a broad knowledge of IT concepts as well as comprehensive skills in handling IT problems. Hopefully, information technology as a profession will eventually adopt a standardized approach to training to define such individuals by rigid criteria. Other professions have established such criteria, and I expect one day the same will happen to IT management. Until that time, the best approach is to search for an IT manager who has vast generalized knowledge as well as experience in a variety of situations.

The Maze of Certifications

For many professions, a legally recognized organization provides a means by which quality training among individuals can be measured. For example, attorneys must pass bar exams, and most physicians must be certified by passing board exams. Unfortunately, this is not the case in the IT industry...at least not yet. Though many organizations are jockeying for such a position, a single authoritative IT organization or examination is not available. Instead, a plethora of vendor-specific certifications exists, and many of these do not necessarily identify the knowledgeable and skillful individuals in the group. Simply because someone has an alphabet soup of initials after his or her name does not mean that the person is qualified to be an information technology manager or systems security person.

Certifications that have been around for a while include the Microsoft Certified Systems Engineer (MCSE) certification and the Cisco Certified Internetwork Expert (CCIE) certification. Both of these are widely recognized within the industry as examinations that define a degree of competency. The MCSE encompasses a total of six examinations on different aspects of Microsoft technologies. Each exam costs between $100 and $200, and preparation courses for these exams are available.

Interestingly, the MCSE and many other certification exams allow individuals to "challenge" the exams without having prior experience or having successfully completed the coursework. This means professionals can simple cram for the exam and take it. If they pass, they receive certification. If not, they can retake the exams again repeatedly, as most do not have limitations in the number of attempts allowed.

The CCIE offered by Cisco is a lot more rigorous. This certification process requires a successful completion of a series of examinations arranged in a hierarchy. One cannot take the next certification exam unless the prior one is successfully mastered. In addition, the CCIE requires completion of a hands-on practical examination offered in limited locations worldwide. Certification is awarded only after all exams and the practical are successfully passed. The CCIE curriculum is one of the few certification processes that have a practical exam component. For this reason and the fact that exams must be taken in sequence, the CCIE certification is currently one of the hardest to attain. As a result, it is revered among the numerous types of IT certifications available.

Outside of these certifications, the remainder varies significantly within the information technology field. Many are vendor-specific, offering little application to the broad range of IT knowledge areas. Others are very general and cover an array of topics but in little depth. Many certifications also cost substantial amounts of money. One virtualization software certification not only requires an exam but also the completion of a course that costs around $3,000. Does this mean these certifications are any better than the rest? Not necessarily. Like many certifying entities, financial incentives as well as business-related incentives exist that favor the development of vendor-specific examinations. Until a professional entity that oversees quality standards in IT knowledge and skills is created, the plethora of certification exams will likely continue.

When you assess IT certifications, consider those that have written and practical exam components; these are preferable to those that do not. Practical exam components require application skills in addition to knowledge, which is important for an organization looking to hire an IT professional. This also eliminates IT professionals who simply cram over a weekend to pass a written exam without truly acquiring the knowledge or skills. Some companies even hire test-taking individuals to memorize and record exam questions so that they can subsequently sell the questions online. Certifications can thus be obtained without merit by those who receive a copy of certification questions and answers.

As mentioned previously, training that involves both knowledge and skill is important. Certifications that test both of these areas are also important. And periodic re-certifications are preferred in any industry that is rapidly changing. Continuing education is a must for the information technology field, and re-certification allows someone to demonstrate proficiency and relevancy in the latest technologies and information. For any one navigating the maze of IT certifications, these are the criteria by which some reasonable assessment of abilities can be performed.

A Need for Soft Skills among IT Personnel

When I was growing up, the stereotypical image of a "techie" was someone who wore thick eyeglasses, a pocket protector with more than enough writing devices, and clothes that combined an offensive array of colors that didn't match. In essence, a techie's excessive intellect came with a cost…a lack of social and interpersonal skills. This image is indeed a stereotype, but in my experience the majority of IT professionals do have a relative deficiency in social savvy. Perhaps this is a natural phenomenon for technically minded people whose right brain overrides their left. Regardless, the need for better communication skills among IT professionals cannot be overstated.

Many IT managers with whom I interact spend nearly 100 percent of their attention and focus on the health of their servers and networks. While this is an important aspect of their jobs, a more significant aspect is being neglected. Ultimately, servers and networks serve people. The users of the network and the clients of the organization should be the primary focus of IT managers. IT systems provide a means by which people's lives are made easier and by which personal productivity is increased. If a server and network is operating perfectly but users are unable to understand their functionality or fail to interact with the IT system in a meaningful way, the IT manager has essentially failed.

IT managers must have strong soft skills if an organization is to thrive. But how do people with strong technical skills suddenly embrace their social sides? Like anything else, the development of skills requires training, education, and practice. Training and continuing education have been described for IT concepts in preceding sections; similarly, training and education in how to relate to people, how to lead individuals, and how to create team incentives can be taught to IT managers. Leadership development, organizational skills, project management, and time management are just a few of the larger areas of education that should be routinely addressed by IT management staff. Mentoring programs as well as feedback assessments are additional tools that help foster greater soft skills. Simply because these skills do not come naturally does not mean that they cannot be learned.

Soft skills help IT personnel relate to the end-user of the IT network and help the organization reach its customers and clients in a more meaningful way. These skills also encourage greater connectivity among organizational departments and help the entire organization adopt unified goals and visions. During many IT consultations and assessments, I have encountered IT departments that have been isolated from the rest of the organization. Barriers in interpersonal communications and differences in departmental goals between the IT department and the rest of the organization can limit the opportunities for success for the entire organization. If no effort is made to help bridge these gaps, problems and challenges ultimately arise as a result.

Effective budget planning is commonly affected by a lack of soft skills among IT managers as well. A budget allowance for the IT department is often absent in an organization. While many reasons may account for this omission, IT managers who have poor communication skills play a role. Their inability to effectively sell themselves and their departments' needs result in a lack of budgetary allowances for IT development and maintenance. Those with strong soft skills are better able to communicate the need for IT budgets. For example, the ability to align declining profits to outdated IT infrastructure or to define increased risk assessments with IT deficiencies allows executive staff to understand needs in organizational terms. No longer does the executive "C-staff" (CEO, CFO, CTO, CIO…) see IT as simply a drain on expenses each year. Instead, they see IT as an integral partner in achieving an organization's goals and fulfilling the organization's mission.

When IT budgets are cut, the first items struck are often training and certification allowances. These cuts save immediate dollars but are not without significant long-term risks. The next common budgetary items cut are IT updates in hardware and software. These save expenses in the short run but do little to save money over the long run and may actually increase costs in downtime and productivity. IT managers who have soft skills can communicate these risks more effectively to those who make budget decisions. If such IT professionals are hard to find, investing in social training and development programs and/or the use of outside consultants may be a good solution.

The bottom line is that IT professionals need stronger communication skills in order to be effective in their roles as organization managers. These skills benefit not only the IT user but also the organization's customers. Additionally, these skills help create teamwork and align efforts toward unified goals throughout the organization. Seeking these individuals and investing in the development in such skills are activities that can certainly serve an organization well.

Responsibilities of the C-Suite

When talking about information technology, focusing on the technology aspect of IT is natural and intuitive. But IT is no longer an island unto itself. IT should be an integral part of any organization today if it wants to compete. And while the skills and knowledge of the IT staff are a large part of a successful IT department, an organization's C-suite of business executives also share IT responsibilities. Many organizations have not recognized this important part of their information management activities, and as a result, gaps in communication develop, limiting productivity and success. Just as IT managers can develop better social and business skills, executives can develop better knowledge of IT.

Many larger organizations have realized this simple fact. Chief technology officers (CTOs) often take a seat next to the CEOs and

CFOs during executive meetings. Their role is to communicate the IT needs of the organization in conjunction with the goals, visions, and mission. All too often, however, CTOs are simply the IT managers with the most seniority, and as previously discussed, their lack of business knowledge and soft skills limit their abilities. Instead of selecting a CTO based on seniority and IT experience alone, you should take into consideration other factors. For example, someone with an MBA degree in addition to IT training and experience can offer greater proficiency in business forecasting and budgeting than someone who has simply managed servers and networks all his or her professional life.

The goal here is to enhance communications between the technical side and the business-management side. A well-qualified CTO can go a long way in this regard. Additionally, initiative taken by other executives to understand and comprehend how information technology relates to business directives should be commonplace in today's high-tech environments. Many executives who lack good technical knowledge may view IT departments simply as budgetary drains. An investment in IT education as it relates to their businesses is a wise choice, and executives will see how IT systems actually increase profitability, productivity, and efficiency.

If these steps can be taken, better communication between the IT department and the executive staff can occur. Likewise, regular communications between the executive branch and the IT department in the form of reports and periodic meetings is a must in order to assess effectiveness and shortcomings. If an organization or an IT department is too busy putting out fires because of endless urgencies and emergencies, these routine communications can get pushed back or neglected altogether. Before long, communication breakdowns occur, and the climate of productivity declines. Efforts to maintain effective communications are imperative, and the executive team certainly shares in this responsibility.

Outsourcing as an Alternative

A relative of mine is a general-practice physician who is very good and understands a great deal about medicine in depth. However as good as he is, I know he does not know the latest and greatest about every medical discovery and treatment for every single bodily system. If I were to have a complex problem with my heart, I am confident he would refer me to a cardiologist for a more detailed assessment. The field is simply too overwhelming for any one person to know everything there is to know.

While many organizations think about outsourcing as a replacement for in-house services, they should also view outsourcing as a means to conduct a thorough assessment of their organizations in particular areas. Like medicine, changes and developments in information technology are quite vast and are occurring at a rapid pace. Even the best IT consultants or managers cannot know everything about the current state of information technology. For this reason, utilizing outside IT consultants provides a supplement to in-house IT personnel. I personally recommend that all organizations have external IT assessments or annual checkups just to be sure that their IT system is the best it can be.

As an IT consultant, I have served this role for many organizations. On some occasions I have identified problem areas and recommended solutions that the organization agreed to implement over a period of time. Unfortunately, these plans for implementation are occasionally neglected, and nothing is resolved. I often suggest a brief follow-up meeting to ensure plans turn into actions. If I arrive for the follow-up meeting and nothing has been done, this in itself is a wake-up call that outside IT services are required.

Of course, many organizations are simply too small to require an in-house IT manager or professional. As a cost-saving measure, outsourcing IT services to a consultant is an ideal option. I perform this function for several smaller organizations, and my title has become a "technology advisor" for these organizations. Assessments can be done weekly, monthly, quarterly, or even annually, depending on the needs of the organization. Over time, a trusting relationship develops, and the efficiency of service is as good as if an in-house person were present. As long as good IT processes are in place and recommendations are acted upon, outsourcing such needs can be very effective.

Selecting a consultant can be a challenge. My consulting business has grown simply by word of mouth and client referrals, and I believe that this is the best approach to finding a good IT professional. Asking friends and colleagues if they have had positive experiences with any specific IT consultant can guide you in the right direction most of the time. Because a high degree of trust as well as confidence must exist in this relationship, positive referrals from others offer greater reliability in finding a consultant who will mesh well with your organization. While simply looking through the Yellow Pages or professional directories are alternative means of searching for an IT expert, testimonials of good service cannot be replaced.

In anticipating the costs of outsourcing IT consultation, realize that fees vary tremendously within the industry. Some consultants offer low fees, but often, discounted prices equal poor service. On the other hand, high fees do not guarantee a quality professional. Charges cannot be reliably used in choosing an IT consultant. At the same time, costs should not be a deterrent. In my experience, the time and cost of a consultation have always been worth the investment. With every consult, a pearl of wisdom and/or identification of a significant problem have been revealed in the process of performing the IT assessment. Over the long run, the amount of money saved in lost productivity, reduced efficiency, and reduced opportunity is substantial compared to the cost of IT outsourcing.

People Make the Difference

Regardless of the nature of your organization, it exists to enhance human life. People make the difference. This focus should permeate not only your business actions and plans but also the IT department. If attention is awarded only on the basis of how well technology is functioning without user benefits, little has been gained. A people-first approach must always be considered. In order to make this goal a reality, IT professionals should have the soft skills needed to communicate well with others. This not only includes customers and users within the organization but also executives who determine IT budgets and strategies.

Additionally, executives have a responsibility to seek IT professionals with good people skills while personally investing in learning the core IT concepts that facilitate business success. In order to bridge the gaps between the technical IT side and the social business side, both parties must compromise. In doing so, goals and missions can be aligned and common values shared. The IT department and management staff should not be operating independently of the rest of the organization but must be important cogs in the wheel that contribute to the entire organization's function. Having the right people in place, whether they are in-house or outsourced, is the key.

CHAPTER 7

Maintenance and Prevention: Avoiding the Fires

We are collectively and individually realizing that resources are indeed limited. The quality of the air we breathe is being threatened by rising levels of carbon gases and pollutants. Climate stability is at risk from the demands of human activity. Even respected scientists predict scarcity of water for human consumption in the future. All resources, including those we have taken for granted throughout human existence, have a finite capacity. This unfortunately also applies to human capital, human resources, and human energy.

Because of our limited energy resources, we must wisely choose how we utilize our energy. Efforts can be invested in proactive solutions that build a better and brighter future, or energy can be spent trying to simply maintain the status quo. When organizations choose to ignore long-term needs, the result is a shift in efforts toward short-term problems. Instead of preventing emergencies and catastrophes by anticipating future needs, energies and resources are consumed trying to put out fires day after day. In my experience, this is particularly true for information technology departments within most organizations.

Information technologies change rapidly. Technologies effective this year may not be as effective the next year or may be incompatible with recently developed technologies. Money spent today on IT is perceived as a poor investment because the same technology next year may be significantly less in cost. As a result, a decision is made to use existing technologies as long as possible until a problem necessitates their replacement. IT is also poorly understood by many business executives and owners. Between a genuine lack of appreciation of IT's value by executives and a lack of effective communication between executives and IT managers, decisions are made to defer IT investments in favor of other interests. A better understanding of IT's benefits to the entire organization would clearly change this tendency.

A few organizational processes should be put in place in order to appreciate the true value of information management. Preventative and maintenance programs can not only avoid costly emergencies and IT failures but can also enhance productivity, efficiency, and organizational value. Ultimately, these programs allow a better use of energy investment among the organization's individuals. The results are exponential in value rather than simply being cumulative. With a slight shift in paradigms, organizations can change the way they approach their IT needs and soon enjoy greater success. The key is to allocate energies toward good IT maintenance rather than wasting resources in disaster management.

Periodic IT Assessments

Regular checkups are an important maintenance procedure for organizations to implement. An organization that performs periodic IT assessments can often anticipate potential problems well in advance. For example, shrinking storage capacity among the organization's servers can be addressed before precious data is lost, or a single failed backup system can be identified before all backup safety nets are affected. An IT assessment provides an overall view of how well an information technology system is currently working and predicts its functional ability into the near future. As a result, components can be added, changed, or enhanced during times of low stress without any interruption in operations.

Periodic IT assessments also inform an organization of the overall quality of its IT tools and technologies. Technologies installed three years ago may no longer be the latest and greatest and may not allow an organization to be competitive in today's environment. Innovative IT strategies may have been developed since an existing IT system was configured that could further improve information technology operations. Without a periodic assessment, an organization will never realize these shortcomings. Therefore, IT assessments can be viewed as both a means to troubleshoot problems in advance as well as ways to ensure that the most effective technology is in place. These proactive efforts offer the best value for an organization while utilizing the least amount of resources and energy.

The frequency with which periodic assessments should be performed depends on several factors, including the size of the organization's IT system, the rate of growth and development, and the presence or absence of routine replacement procedures. In general, the larger the organization and the faster the rate of change, the more frequent an IT assessment should be. For some organizations, annual IT assessments may be satisfactory, while others may require quarterly or even monthly assessments. Over time, IT assessment frequencies may vary as well. Infrequent evaluations may have been ideal previously, but because of rapid organizational growth, more-frequent assessments may now be required.

Some organizations, especially larger organizations with complex IT systems, prefer to use in-house IT managers to conduct periodic IT assessments. However, I generally recommend outside consultation to be involved in some of the assessments. Having an outside IT consultant examine the IT system offers a fresh perspective from a professional with a wide array of experience and knowledge. While in-house IT managers may have great resumes, they essentially deal with the same IT infrastructure, tools, and technologies day after day. A consultant, on the other hand, has the chance to see hundreds of different IT configurations and equipment pieces at a variety of different organizations each year. Even if outside consultants perform a fraction of the periodic assessments, the investment is certainly worthwhile.

Monitoring Implementation

Conducting an IT assessment is great in terms of identifying the needs of an organization, but little is gained from the assessment if proposed plans are never implemented. Steps must be taken to ensure that the recommendations from the assessment come to fruition. Otherwise, the resources already invested are wasted. As a means to hold itself accountable, an organization should have some type of procedure in place to monitor progress as well as to ensure completion of these IT projects and changes. Ticketing systems and meetings between IT managers and executives are some examples of these checks and balances, but other options exist.

Project management professionals are among the most sought-after positions in the IT field. By setting goals, defining milestones, coordinating team efforts, and enhancing communications, project management professionals facilitate implementation while using as few resources as possible. Not only can they monitor whether IT plans are being implemented, but they can also manages the implementation more efficiently and at a reduced cost compared to simple delegation of tasks. If an IT assessment identifies a shortcoming, a project to resolve the problem is defined. From here, a project manager and team oversee progress and make sure the project goes to completion as planned. Regular meetings by the team and communications with executive staff hold the project manager and team members accountable along the way.

Of course, some organizations are not large enough to employ full project management services with a project manager. In these circumstances, IT managers may be solely responsible for implementing changes and completing projects. But what happens if these managers fail to follow through on the commitment? I have consulted with many organizations in which the IT manager was too busy handling emergencies and had little to no time to perform maintenance activities. Unfortunately, this becomes a vicious cycle as emergencies prevent routine maintenance, and this in turn leads to more emergencies. In these circumstances, outside consultation can help provide a comprehensive perspective on what is truly happening in the organization. At a minimum, a consultant can provide IT services temporarily to help get the organization back on the right track.

In environments in which IT personnel are too busy to monitor project completion, regular use of outside experts is a great way to ensure continued quality while limiting the expense of the investment. Even if a consultant is needed once a month, the costs are far less than the expense of handling IT disasters and the loss of revenue from failed business continuity. Mechanisms that ensure that plans are actually getting done should be a priority for any organization. Whether these mechanisms are handled within the organization or with the assistance of outside expertise, monitoring project completion is a necessary process to promote success.

Aligning Corporate and IT Goals

From a conceptual standpoint, every business and organization has values, goals, and missions. Typically these are overarching qualities that define the organization and guide it through growth and development. Many times, specific departments within an organization may fail to align themselves with the organization's defining criteria, which ultimately results in mismatches and inefficiencies. For example, the human resources department may fail to hire individuals who reflect the goals, values, and mission of the organization. Once in their assigned positions, these individuals are unable to fulfill the true needs of the organization, and the direction of growth and development becomes askew.

Because many executives poorly understand IT in general and because IT managers notoriously lack strong social and communication skills, a gap in understanding between an organization and its IT department often causes poor alignment between the IT department and stated corporate values. An organization may list its mission as providing quality customer service in sales and support, yet the IT infrastructure may fail to accommodate these needs. Poor documentation abilities, inefficient communications, and interrupted continuity could all undermine the comprehensive desires of an organization.

All departments within an organization should make sure that they consider global directives of the organization when developing their individual department activities. Because IT plays such an integral role in smooth operations in today's business climate, proper alignment of IT procedures, technologies, and tools with the organization's goals, values, and mission is imperative. Without this alignment, success is much harder to achieve. How can one expect employees to meet the organization's standards if the right tools are not available for the task? IT in particular provides personnel with the right platform by which people can fulfill the organization's standards.

As part of the enhanced communication process, executive members of an organization and IT personnel must have the same vision when devising proper information technology systems. Discussions about risk management, business continuity, and disaster recovery are all included in these communications as well as issues surrounding how IT can help the organization achieve its mission and goals. If this cannot be accomplished internally, external consultation once again may provide assistance and direction. Regardless, the more aligned an IT system is with the overriding directives of the organization, the higher will be the chance of organizational success.

Developing a Knowledge Base and Promoting Organizational Learning

Knowledge bases and organizational learning are relatively new concepts for businesses and organizations; while these areas do not solely belong to information technologies, IT provides the tools and infrastructure needed to foster these activities. Developing a knowledge base within an organization can vary from data collection of ticketing complaints to information gathered through IT assessments, surveys, and a host of other organizational activities. Almost every organization has a significant amount of data whether it realizes it or not. The key is to capture, organize, and catalog this data so that it becomes a useful tool for the organization. IT systems are the means by which this can be accomplished.

Organizational learning on the other hand has to do with processes and procedures in place that allow more-effective and more-efficient operations. A monitoring procedure for the implementation of project plans is an example of such a process. As the organization understands how these processes can be streamlined and made more effective, learning occurs. The same learned concepts can then be applied to other processes in the organization when applicable. IT systems can provide the means by which such learning is recorded and cataloged. When a new procedure or process needs to be developed, retrieving data from other processes in place can offer the most effective solutions.

Information technologies can facilitate organizational knowledge and learning simply by creating methods by which information is systematically collected and stored. Systems that are able to tag and catalog data make retrieval simple and efficient. Imagine that a marketing department plans to launch a campaign to promote a new product. While market research and consumer demographics provide a great deal of information about a particular consumer group, an abundance of information is also available internally about past customers and performance of past marketing campaigns. If a knowledge base is readily accessible, a better marketing strategy can be developed. This saves a great deal of time in information gathering and raises the chances of an effective campaign.

Examples of how knowledge bases can assist in IT troubleshooting have been described in the discussion of ticketing and logging systems in Chapter 5. However, IT processes can be used to gather and organize any data that an organization wishes to capture. This investment in data management will pay significant dividends in the long term as less energy will be spent in information search and application. Creating a knowledge base and promoting organizational learning is simply another way to get the most out of an IT system.

Fireproofing Versus Firefighting

In 2004, three years after 9/11, local, state and federal representatives met as part of a planning exercise to assess emergency disaster management abilities should a major hurricane strike the coastal areas of Louisiana. The exercise, named "Hurricane Pam," considered the problems and response abilities should a Category 5 Hurricane strike (REF 4). The representatives found multiple shortcomings. Communication infrastructure was poor. Transportation capacity compared to population needs was markedly limited. Health and rescue services were inadequate to handle anticipated human services. At the conclusion of the exercise, plans were devised and members accepted responsibilities in an effort to correct these deficiencies. However, a year later, when Hurricane Katrina struck, little had been accomplished. Thousands of lives were lost or affected as a result of a lack of implementation. When the imagined crisis became a reality, preventative measures had been neglected, and the response to the catastrophe was far from acceptable.

While lives are rarely at stake for most organizations, a lack of preparedness and prevention is all too common. Maintenance of IT systems is ignored or neglected. Adoption of better technologies and tools does not happen due to financial costs or a lack of understanding. As a result, IT systems suffer more-frequent and more-significant problems over time, demanding immediate attention from IT personnel. In the process, business continuity is disrupted, revenues and customers are lost, and efforts are used inefficiently in attending to disaster management. Choosing to be proactive and adopt preventative measures is a simple solution that effectively minimizes these unwanted developments.

Information technology systems are a necessary component of organizations and businesses today. This book has described a smart approach to installing an effective IT infrastructure with proper technologies and tools as well as the importance of having the right IT professionals. Also, a commitment to ongoing monitoring of IT systems is mandatory if success is the goal in a competitive environment. Periodic assessments, oversight of project completions, alignment of goals between IT and the organization, and the development of an internal knowledge base are examples of this commitment. In this way, resource investments can be used wisely and most effectively.

Fireproofing your information technology system is no different than reducing risk in other areas of an organization. Organizations are always more productive and efficient when unnecessary stress is absent. For organizations that are in a cycle of putting out fire after fire, not only is productivity affected by interruptions in business continuity, but it is also hindered because of the stressful pressure of the situation. By applying the IT concepts in this book to your organization, you can reduce the times of stress experienced and maximize the fluency of business operations. This does not require you to understand every single aspect of your IT system; it requires only open dialogue, good communications, and a commitment to establishing smart IT processes and procedures. With these attitudes in place, organizational success becomes more likely. After all, IT should be an asset, not a liability, for your organization. Stop running from fire to fire, and make the choice to invest in good IT practices.

References

4   Hurricane Pam Exercise: http://en.wikipedia. org/wiki/Hurricane_preparedness_for_New_Orleans

INDEX

T
Ticketing 65-66
Tower Server 40
Training 70-71

U
UPS 59-60
Uninterruptible Power Supply
    59-60

V
VLAN 50-51
VM 42-43
VPN 49
Virtual Private Network 49
Virtual Local Area Network
    50-51
Virtual Machine 42-43
Virtualization 42-43

W
WAN 48
Wiki 67
Workstation 43-44

ABOUT THE AUTHOR

With over twenty years experience in information technology, David Papp is recognized as one of the foremost experts in network and security solutions. David has provided consultative services for organizations, from small companies to large corporations, throughout the world and enjoys architecting high-performance networks geared toward success. He also serves as a regular keynote speaker sharing his expertise on IT topics throughout the United States and Canada for a wide variety of audiences.

David's experience dates back to the 1980s, when he began his own IT services company as a teenager. In the early 1990s, he created one of the first local Internet home pages and later founded one of Canada's Internet service providers. Equipped with years of experience in IT developments, a computer engineering degree from the University of Alberta, and a profound understanding of IT networking and security, David is well respected among clients and colleagues from around the world.

David resides in Alberta, Canada, where he is a registered professional engineer and operates his international consulting business. He also holds a number of industry-related certifications, including Cisco, Microsoft, and VMware, among others. In addition to having an active professional career, he enjoys travelling and outdoor activities with his family.